Don't Nag ... *TAG!*

Success the First Time with TAGteach®

Theresa McKeon

Don't Nag ... TAG!

TAGteach.com
Theresa McKeon: t@TAGteach.com
Joan Orr: joan@TAGteach.com

ISBN-13: 978-1-7320975-1-3

www.529books.com
Editor: Lisa Cerasoli
Interior: Lauren Michelle
Cover: Claire Moore

Praise for *Don't Nag ... TAG!*

"TAGteach is going to change the way I teach for the rest of my career. I recommend this training to everybody. The students are self-correcting because they either hear the tag or they don't, which is where the true learning happens."

Cheryl Anderson
Director of Instruction, Mike Bender Golf Academy
2006 National LPGA Teacher of the Year

"TAGteach has brought the essence of basic behavioral research to practical application in widely divergent areas of human development, including education, corporate training, athletic coaching, industrial safety, and even orthopedic surgery. The extent to which the Founders of this movement have been able to continuously adapt, improve, and apply this simplistic approach to new and different populations and applications is stunning."

Dr. Carl Binder
CEO, The Performance Thinking Network, LLC
Seattle, Washington

"Something that has aided your little girl to walk when others said she never would.... Something that has helped your little girl engage with her environment, one she hardly used to take notice of.... How do you explain the feeling of sheer joy as your little girl's sensory meltdown turns into laughs and giggles before your very eyes? There are no words. TAGteach is our family's champion."

Sean Pogson
Parent of a child with Autism
United Kingdom

"TAGteach is simply the most effective strategy we have used to teach our residents surgical tool skills. This is going to change forever how the medical industry trains its personnel."

I. Martin Levy, MD
Program Director and Clinical Professor of Orthopaedic Surgery
Albert Einstein College of Medicine, Montefiore Medical Center
New York City, New York

"B. F. Skinner believed that his science would promote human welfare. TAGteach exemplifies this belief and would have pleased him immensely."

Julie S. Vargas, PhD
President, B.F. Skinner Foundation
Author of *Behavior Analysis for Effective Teaching*
Boston, Massachusetts

"I love everything about TAGteach. I love the tag, I love the positive reinforcement. I love no negative connotations. I love the focus on what *I* need to do. I love everything about it and I plan on using it extensively in my teaching."

Grant Grinnell
Tennis Instructor
USPTA (United States Professional Tennis Association)
Seattle Washington

"TAGteach is an incredibly powerful tool for teaching mechanical skills to blind and visually impaired learners. I would recommend TAGteach become a part of every teacher's toolbox."

Michele Pouliot
Director of Research and Development, Guide Dogs for the Blind
Portland, Oregon

"Wow! You have succeeded in getting people to minimize and control verbal instruction more effectively than anyone I know."

Bethan Mair Williams
Specialist Speech and Language Therapist/BCBA
Chair Founder of Royal College of Speech and Language Therapy Clinical Excellence Network
Wales, UK

"Imagine a camp full of teenagers where they never have to be nagged to do dishes, everyone helps everyone else, they pick up after themselves, and everyone is prepared for their activities. It sounds like magic, but, really, it's TAGteach in action."

Abigail Curtis and Karin Coyne
Owners/Founders of Adventure Unleashed
Reynoldsburg, Ohio

Table of Contents

Don't Nag ... TAG!
Success the First Time with TAGteach®

1 For the Millionth Time...

> "There is no easy way to train an apprentice.
> My two tools are example and nagging."
>
> *Lemony Snicket: "Who Could That Be at This Hour?"*

1.1 Toes, Toes, Toes, Toes, Toes

As you walk onto the floor of a large sports arena, you can't help but feel like a gladiator, destined to succeed or fail on an epic scale.

Although I was walking in as a coach and not a competitor, I wasn't immune to the adrenaline rush. At this level of competition, stakes are high for everyone. Athletes compete against each other—and by extension, their coaches do too. Everyone is on edge when perfection is the goal.

At this meet, as was typical before large competitions, teams were broken apart by age and level, and regrouped with members of other teams for warmups. This gives athletes an opportunity to test the equipment and coaches a chance to briefly greet one another and subtly size up their opposition. I was handed the schedule during registration and saw that we were in the same rotation as a very well-known team and their equally well-known coach.

Once our athletes were set up and working, I decided to pay homage to this coach. "Your girls look great. What's your secret?"

She continued focusing on her tiny athlete flipping down the balance beam. I took her silence as a hint to move along. But before I turned to walk away, she yelled, "Anna! Toes, toes, toes, toes, toes, toes, toes! Point them or go home!" Then she pointed at me (quite violently if I recall) and said, "You want my secret? That's my secret!" She paused, but I didn't respond, which was good because she wasn't finished. "I just nag and nag and nag and nag and nag and nag." Before I could think of something more intelligent than "Oh," the coach charged between a landscape of springboards to another athlete, apparently in need of nagging.

Huh? Not exactly the holy grail of coaching I was expecting. Why did a coach with such experience and success rely on nagging as a coaching methodology?

In truth, I had a tremendous amount of expertise with nagging in its various forms. But somehow hearing it from this professional, in this arena, under these spotlights, "nagging" just seemed absurd.

- Why, especially in athletics, when time is of the essence, do we choose to repeat instructions that have already failed? "I've told you a million times to point your toes."

- Why do we use nagging as a parenting strategy? "I've told you a million times to put your homework in your backpack when you're finished, so you're not rushing around in the morning."

- Why do bosses nag their employees? "I've asked the managers a million times to be more proactive with their staff."

"Hey," one of the other coaches said. "Your girl is up."

Embarrassing—I was so wrapped up in my thoughts that I'd lost track of the lineup. I transferred the blame and yelled, "Stephanie, you're up, let's go!"

Stephanie jumped up on the beam, threw a few skills, and then finished with her dismount. As she landed, a flash of color caught my eye. She stuck the landing, and even maintained the elusive pointed toes, but it was her pink nail polish that grabbed my attention the most.

I yelled for her to come over. "For crying out loud, Stephanie! You can't wear pink nail polish during a major competition—I've told you that a million times!"

1.2 Nagging—Logical Progression

Teachers do it. Coaches do it. Leaders do it. Parents do it. And everyone hates to be on the receiving end of it.

So why do we nag? Turns out, it's a logical progression of the tools we've been given:

- give the learner instructions;
- if the learner doesn't follow those instructions;
- repeat the instructions.

With each repetition, the same instructions may get louder, or be delivered with more intensity. In a worst-case scenario, nagging can even be dangerous. I learned just how dangerous, not from coaching gymnasts, but from Romeo.

1.3 Romeo, oh, Romeo

At six years old, I fell in love with Shoshone. He was a spunky pony that took care of me during the riding portion of summer camp. It was the whole trite story. Girl sees pony; girl falls in love with pony; girl wants pony to live in her room.

Thirty years later, this girl was finally in the position to buy her own pony. You would think that two years of summer camp would've provided plenty of experience for purchasing a horse, but no.

First rookie mistake: When buying horses, as with many things, you get what you pay for. I did not pay enough for this horse.

Second rookie mistake: I bought Romeo (a perfect name as he was so handsome) without an experienced horse person to advise me. I met with a shady horse trader, who drugged Romeo just enough to make him seem like a dream horse. He was not. After the drugs wore off, I couldn't get Romeo to accept a rider. Yelling, pleading, even trying to be "nice" did nothing. He just seemed to lose his mind when anyone got in the saddle. I had no business owning this horse.

Third rookie mistake: I hired Chuck, a self-proclaimed cowboy, to help me with Romeo. Over the phone, he'd told me, "Don't worry. I've fixed hundreds of these spoiled horses."

(Note: my mistakes pile high in this story, so I'll quit numbering them now.)

Chuck the cowboy agreed to come out to the barn that day. While I waited for him to arrive, I saddled Romeo and led him out to a small, round pen. On the ground, I felt perfectly safe with Romeo. He was a big love bug as long as you weren't on his back.

A few minutes later, I saw a dusty truck pull up the driveway. I yelled, "We're back here!"

Chuck got out of his truck, and with cowboy hat in hand, sauntered over. "Okay, little lady, let's see what we got here."

He motioned for me to get up in the saddle. I did—slowly.

"Well, get him going, girl," he said.

I took a deep breath, held it, and asked Romeo to walk forward. Romeo declined.

'Kick 'em!" Chuck said insistently.

I asked Romeo to walk forward with my voice, then with my seat, and then with a delicate kick to his sides. He declined each time.

"Kick 'em again—harder! Harder! Yank those reigns! Turn him in a circle. Kick! Kick! Kick! Eventually he'll get tired of fighting and just do it."

Nope. I could guarantee that wasn't going to happen. Romeo was an old-type Morgan, which, by definition, meant he was never going to tire. What he *was* going to do was gather up a head of steam and dump me.

"I can't kick any harder, and if I yank those reigns again, he's gonna blow!"

The look on Chuck's face said it all—I didn't have the physical or mental toughness needed to get this done. "I think it would be best if Romeo came to my place and I can fix him there," he said.

Yes, please! At this point, I was too scared, frustrated, and inexeperienced to make good decisions. I was relieved to get out of the saddle and literally turn the reigns over to someone else. But as we walked back to Chuck's trailer and loaded Romeo inside, I said, "He didn't blow today because we stopped, but I want to warn you: when Romeo wants you off his back, you'll be off."

"Don't you worry, little lady. Just let me handle him."

The very next day I received a phone call. The man on the phone was not Chuck, but a friend of his calling to let me know Romeo was on his way home.

"Why?" I asked. Turns out Romeo had violently thrown Chuck to the ground, and he'd been taken to the hospital with three cracked bones.

"Is he okay? What can I do? How can I help?"

His friend explained that, although it sounded bad, Chuck was already home from the hospital and would make a full recovery. He was calling to assure me that Chuck wanted nothing from me, and nothing more to do with Romeo.

An hour later, a truck and horse trailer turned onto my driveway. A man stepped out, lowered the ramp to the trailer, and stood back—way back. Romeo rumbled out, looking no worse for the wear.

I tried apologizing again but was met with silence as the man handed me the lead rope attached to Romeo, slammed the trailer ramp closed, got back in the truck, and disappeared down the road.

Although it would not absolve me, I did think, *I told you so.*

1.4 Don't Piss off a Whale—Then Jump in the Water with It

Nothing short of desperation made me think I could succeed where experts had failed. To keep anyone else from being injured, I'd have to find a way to train Romeo myself.

I reached out to the internet for information. Search engines were just becoming user-friendly in 1997. Anyone could type in a few keywords and hundreds of related articles would pop up on the screen. I think I typed in: *How do you train a horse that wants to kill you?*

The search led me to an article on training killer whales at Sea World. The staff never physically punished the whales. That seemed perfectly reasonable, as it doesn't bode well to smack a killer whale on the nose and then jump in the water with it. Instead, they were using a formal protocol that included positive reinforcement.

The term *positive reinforcement* was used in a very specific context. When the whale did something correctly, the trainer would use a whistle to identify or "mark" the exact moment of success. The whistle was also a bridge between 1) doing the correct thing and, 2) receiving positive reinforcement upon returning to the trainer. A connection between "the sound of the whistle" and "good things" was made. A strong relationship between the trainer and the whale was also being cultivated.

But this type of training wasn't just for marine mammals. Trainers in the horse world[1] and the dog world[2] were finding success as well. *Bingo!* If I could learn to use this positive reinforcement technique, maybe Romeo and I had a chance.

1.5 It Just Clicked

I whittled the information down to three important steps:

1. Divide skills into small pieces—to acquire one at a time.

2. Use an audible mark to indicate success.

3. Provide immediate reinforcement.

---

[1] Alexandra Kurland, https://www.theclickercenter.com/

[2] Karen Pryor, *Don't Shoot the Dog: The New Art of Teaching and Training*

I wanted to give it a try. There was a recommended first "game" to play with your horse, and it didn't involve getting on Romeo's back. That was a plus.

I gathered the items that were needed for Romeo's inaugural clicker training:

- a plastic box clicker (instead of the more difficult to master whistles used by the marine mammal trainers);

- a small red traffic cone to use as a target (something not typically in Romeo's environment that would initially draw his attention);

- a carrot cut into thirty pieces, stuffed into my pocket (something Romeo really loved).

I walked out to the barn, leaned into the half door of his stall, and had a chat with a horse.

"Look, Romeo, I failed big-time with that last training fiasco. If you're up for it, I'd like to try something different."

He continued standing there, occasionally flicking his tail—I took that as a yes.

"All right, let's just play a game. No saddles, no getting on your back—just a game of "touch target."

The end goal was for Romeo to touch the cone with his nose when I asked him to. But this would be done in steps. The instructions were to "click" if he showed any movement toward it, attention to it, or touched it, even accidentally.

The first session looked like this:

The Touch Target Game

I presented the traffic cone about five inches from his face.

I clicked, marking the very second Romeo looked at the cone.

I immediately offered a piece of carrot.

Romeo took it—good.

I presented the cone about a foot from his face.

Romeo stretched his neck out to smell it.

I clicked, then delivered the carrot.

Romeo took it.

I presented the cone about a foot from his face.

Romeo stretched his neck to get a better sensory description and accidentally bumped it with his nose.

I clicked and then offered a piece of carrot.

Romeo took it.

I moved back from the half door with the cone held well within his sight and reach, thinking he would stretch forward to touch it.

Romeo did not.

I revised.

I moved closer to Romeo. Now the cone was less than a foot from his face.

Romeo decided it was still interesting enough to reach out and sniff.

I clicked and then offered a piece of carrot.

Romeo froze.

About three seconds later, he retrieved the carrot from my palm.

I presented the cone.

Romeo reached out, and with purpose, bumped the cone.

I clicked and presented the carrot slice.

Romeo took it, looked away for a brief second, and then looked back at me.

I presented the cone.

Romeo nosed it with even greater intention.

I clicked and offered the carrot piece.

Romeo popped his head up at the sound of the clicker, paused, and lowered his head to take the carrot piece.

We continued to play "touch target" until all thirty pieces of carrot were gone, which took all of three minutes. I showed him my empty hands to assure him the game was over. Then Romeo did something a little unsettling.

While finishing off the remnants of the final carrot, he stared at me— straight into my eyes. Such a rare thing. I imagined he was saying, "I never thought you were intelligent enough to communicate with me. What a pleasant surprise. Let's do this more often. Oh, and I like the whole carrot thing—makes all the extra work communicating with you worthwhile."

We continued playing the clicker game on the ground, and even from the saddle. Each time we needed to clear up our communication, I went back to the click-reinforce protocol. There was no force. There was no fight. Only individual steps toward a common goal. It was a dream come true.

1.6 If You Could Only Do That with People...

A fellow horse enthusiast following our progression was intrigued.

"The change in Romeo is amazing," she said.

Actually, the change was in the teacher. Romeo was simply responding.

Using the clicker training techniques improved my ability to identify and stick to a "one goal at a time" agenda, and to give feedback and positive reinforcement in a more efficient manner.

My friend snickered, "Now if you could only do *that* with your athletes."

We laughed. *Yeah, can you imagine clicking your athletes?*

Then I stopped laughing.

I thought about the steps. This time, from a coach's point of view:

1.   Divide skills into small pieces—to acquire one at a time.

As a coach, I thought I already knew how to break it down (a forward roll on the floor before a front flip in the air), but this was different. I had to pay more attention to the learner than to my lesson plan. I could do that with my athletes.

2.   Use an audible mark to immediately indicate success

The audible marker I used with Romeo was a clicker. Using the clicker instead of my voice was not imperative, but advantageous in the sense that it was faster, salient in the environment, had a single meaning (yes), and didn't carry additional emotional content. I figured that may benefit my human students, too.

3.   Provide positive, timely reinforcement

At first, I thought this meant giving my athletes a food treat after every success, as I did with Romeo. Glad I was wrong. After learning more about the science of reinforcement, it was clear positive reinforcers are determined by the learner. For my athletes, knowing they'd done something correctly at the very instant of performance, (the click) was sure to be positive reinforcement.

These steps were not about using a clicker or training animals. They were about clear communication. This was a technique to improve the teacher.

And a better teacher will create a better learner—no matter the species.

1.7 The Worst That Could Happen Was—Nothing

It wouldn't be so far-fetched to put the three steps I used with Romeo into a lesson plan and give it a try with my gymnasts. What's the worst that could happen? Nothing.

I chose a group of very young gymnasts—they were just learning but could all do a basic handstand. We could tackle "point your toes" before it became a dreaded nag point. I preplanned the three steps:

1. The skill was a handstand, the achievable piece would be "pointed toes."

2. "Pointed toes" would be marked with a clicker. (I chose to use the clicker, as the sound would cut through the ambient noise in the gym. Plus, the clicker was fun.)

3. The reinforcement: I attached value to each click. When a gymnast collected ten clicks, they could be "redeemed" for an ice pop, typically something everyone wanted during a hot, three-hour workout. (This was my carrot.)

I called the trial group over and had the girls line up for instructions.

The Point Your Toes Game

"One at a time, you'll kick up to a handstand. When your toes point at the top, you'll hear a click. That means you win! Collect ten clicks and you can trade them in for an ice pop."

Squeals followed my simple instructions.

"Sarah, you're first."

Sarah kicked up to a handstand. She pointed her toes.

I clicked at the very instant she pointed her toes.

Sarah said, "Yes!"

Jane was up next. She kicked up to a handstand. She pointed her toes.

I clicked.

Jane said, "Yes!"

Jess was up next and eagerly kicked up to a handstand. Jess's toes were not pointed. She stepped out of the handstand and said, "Wait! I have to point my toes." Then she kicked back up to the handstand and pointed her toes.

I clicked, never having to point out the error.

The girls were self-assessing their performance and keeping track of the number of clicks they'd earned.

"I've got five!"

"I've got six!"

The clicks were little packets of information: "You did it!" To an athlete who wants to succeed, success is a great reinforcer.

Ashley asked if she could be the one who clicked. I said, "No," but then thought, *Why not?* If the gymnast can perform the goal, they should be able to identify someone else performing it.

"Okay, Kara, you kick to handstand," I said, handing Ashley the clicker. "Ashley, you click when you see pointed toes."

Kara kicked up to a handstand and pointed her toes.

Ashley clicked.

Both smiled for the win.

The gymnasts wanted to play the clicker game more and more. They would go home and tell their parents, "I got twenty-five today." I couldn't help but think, *When have these athletes ever been told they did something right twenty-five times in one day?*

With donations from the gym owner and even the parents, we set up a store (an unused cupboard) where gymnasts could "buy" items with their collected clicks. They took their time and carefully chose from snacks, athletic tape, crazy pencils, "coupons" for extra rest time, or "choice of music" to be played during the workout. The athletes loved it.

1.8 Clickers Don't Yell, Clickers Don't Get Mad

Although it made perfect sense, the transition from yelling to clicking was awkward for me. When stress was low, I used the three steps. When stress was high, I was quick to abandon them. For me, nagging was a brain saver. I didn't have to stop and figure out why the athlete was still doing a particular movement incorrectly, I could just repeat the instructions I'd given the last time. Overcoming my history with taking the easy way out (nagging) and blaming the learner was going to take some practice.

As it turned out, my practice time with this gymnastics club was coming to an end. My husband was offered a job in a new state and we both liked the idea of an adventure. The decision was made. In a whirlwind, we packed up the kids, the dogs, and the horses, and moved north.

Experienced gymnastic coaches are typically in demand, and I found a new position quickly. But starting in a new gym means acclimating to their culture. Talking about my new three-step teaching method and pulling a clicker out of my pocket would take a lot of explanation. I decided to hold off for a while. And a little while longer. And a little while longer.

Until...

My daughter, a gym rat from the time she could walk, had worked her way up to the competitive level at our new gym. For the first time, I was not only the coach of a competitive athlete, but the mother of one as well. Her workouts increased from three hours a week to ten. As the work got harder, the complaints got louder.

"They don't care that I'm scared," she'd say. "I'm trying, but it doesn't help when they yell at me." Or,

"I don't want to go to practice tonight. I'll just get all stressed out."

Mind you, I was one of the coaches yelling and pushing her. From a mother's point of view, I don't want anyone making my little girl "stressed out." It's supposed to be fun, right? But from the coach's point of view, there isn't a lot of room for whiners in this sport. Get over it or get a new sport.

The cognitive dissonance made me revisit the Romeo scenario. He wasn't a spoiled horse that needed to be fixed. He needed me to be a better teacher. My gymnasts, including my daughter, needed me to be a better teacher. I knew how to do it, I just needed a push.

That push came in the form of an email from a Canadian scientist named Joan Orr. She had read an article I wrote about training athletes with an audible marker (clicker). Joan also had children competing in gymnastics, and a background in clicker training. She, too, was interested in the idea that positive reinforcement and marker-based training could improve coaching outcomes. She asked about my work, and I told her of the successes we'd had. Then I told her I wasn't actively using the clicker in my current facility.

She asked the obvious question. "If it worked so well, why did you stop?"

Why *did* I stop? After all my excuses fell flat, there was only one reason left. I quit because it wasn't as easy as nagging. Nagging was the norm; nagging didn't have to be "explained" or "approved" by the owners of the new facility.

"Okay, why don't you try it again?" she suggested.

It was that simple. Try again. If nothing else, it would help reduce the frustration with my daughter—that alone would be worth the extra effort. I told Joan that I'd bring it up to the management at the next practice.

Luckily, the head coach at the club was very progressive. She was open to anything that improved the training environment and encouraged the girls to stick with the sport. "Give it a try," she said.

But there was a wrinkle.

In the few years since my last foray with the audible marker, clicker training had gone mainstream in the dog-training world. One gymnast wrinkled her nose as she told us, "My mom says this is how they train dogs."

I thought, *Well, if by "this" you mean using positive reinforcement and clear communication to improve skill acquisition and build a trust between student and teacher, then, yes. If you mean because of the clicker, then, no.* You can change out the clicker for any sound or stimulus that quickly and clearly communicates the moment of success. Carefully done, you can even use words like "yes" or "yep" to mark success.

How could we explain to the general public that this three-step process was part of the science of learning for everyone?

Did I mention Joan was a scientist?

"Not a problem," Joan said. "We can kill two birds with one stone."

If I was willing to begin working with the marker-based technique again, Joan said she'd put together a protocol for a study. We could demonstrate the effectiveness and document how the athletes felt about the training.

With permission from the parents, the team owners graciously allowed the study. As expected, the results were stunning. The skills were acquired faster, and the gymnasts had a unique way of telling us they liked using the clicker as an audible marker. "Clickers don't yell at us. Clickers don't get mad."

Now I was energized! I started using the three-step technique again and again, and the team immediately responded. They even helped me stay on course and steer clear of nagging with subtle reminders, "Theresa, you seem a little stressed out, so I got a clicker from the office."

1.9 Teaching with Acoustic Guidance

With Joan Orr's team of Special Olympic rhythmic gymnasts and my team of artistic gymnasts, we spent the next few years testing, modifying, and maturing the technique and developing additional tools. The athletes responded exceptionally well to the audible click because it was clear and didn't overwhelm them with verbal language and emotions. Because the acoustic marker played such an integral role, we formally named our process Teaching with Acoustic Guidance. The acronym TAG stuck, and the entire toolbox became known as TAGteach.

In 2003, Joan and I began sharing our findings with others outside of the gymnastics world. We asked Beth Wheeler, a longtime colleague and owner of her own dance academy, to help us further develop the process with a wider range of learners. She was eager to join. Apparently, dance teachers were equally relieved to have a successful alternative to nagging.

Ultimately, we teamed up with Aaron Clayton and Karen Pryor. Karen is widely known as one of the developers of the original clicker training technique. She had trained dolphins, whales, ponies, dogs, and had done early work with humans. With her guidance and connections to others in the science of behavior, TAGteach continued to evolve.

1.10 Today

Today, people from around the world are using TAGteach to teach, coach, lead, and parent with maximum clarity, while providing instant feedback and timely reinforcement.

Nagging isn't necessary when you have success the first time.

In the following chapters, we'll discuss the methodology and tools used in TAGteach, introduce the process, and share inspiring stories of those who agree: Don't Nag...TAG!

2 TAGteach

If you come in contact with other living beings,

by chance or by choice, you are a teacher.

2.1 What is TAGteach?

TAGteach is a methodology to bring the student and the teacher together—at the moment of learning.

Teachers, coaches, leaders, and parents use TAGteach to create vastly better communication that virtually guarantees their learner will succeed—the first time.

"TAGteach has brought the essence of basic behavioral research to practical application in widely divergent areas of human development, including education, corporate training, athletic coaching, industrial safety, and even orthopedic surgery. The extent to which the Founders of this movement have been able to continuously adapt, improve, and apply this simplistic approach to new and different populations and applications is stunning."

Dr. Carl Binder
CEO, The Performance Thinking Network, LLC

"TAGteach is simply the most effective strategy we have used to teach our residents surgical tool skills. This is going to forever change how the medical industry trains its personnel."

I. Martin Levy, MD
Program Director and Clinical Professor of Orthopaedic Surgery
Albert Einstein College of Medicine
Montefiore Medical Center

TAGteach focuses on the structured application of positive reinforcement and scientifically established principles and practices.[3] Within this framework, the words "behavior" and "reinforce" have specific definitions.

> **Behavior:** For our purposes, a behavior is any observable activity a learner does. The conditions in the environment always influence behavior. Behavior never occurs in a vacuum. Examples of behavior are walking, talking, frowning, reading, eating, speaking, etc. This differs from the more common use of labels for behavior such as smart, stubborn, and competitive.

> **Positive Reinforcement:** Throughout this book, the term "reinforcement" refers only to positive reinforcement. Positive reinforcement is the process of increasing behavior by providing valued consequences to the learner when the desired action is performed.[4] It's important to note we reinforce behavior, not people. We'll talk more about reinforcement in Chapter 5.

The first thing we have to understand in using TAGteach, or when teaching in general, is that "teacher knowledge" covers a far greater scope of any given subject than can be imparted to the learner at any one moment. This inequity can drive us mad and, in that madness, we struggle or resort to nagging.

---

[3] G. David Smith, PhD, BCBA-D, on an explanation of TAGteach™ including: task analysis, shaping by successive approximations, discrimination training, differential reinforcement of alternative responding, errorless discrimination, generalization, behavioral momentum, modeling/imitation, and vicarious reinforcement.

[4] Definition of behavior and positive reinforcement was provided by Susan G. Friedman, PhD, Utah State University and Behavior+ Works

Teacher struggle: "I explained how to do it in great detail many times and he still didn't do it correctly. I'm so frustrated!"

Learner struggle: "I get completely lost every time he goes into those long explanations. I'm so frustrated!"

Now you can eliminate this frustration with a three-step methodology:

Identify—Tag—Reinforce

Together, they form the TAGteach Triangle.

Step 1: Identify the goal

The teacher identifies and delivers a single goal and its well-defined criteria for success. (Detailed in Chapter 3)

Step 2: Tag success

A brief mark (sound, sight, touch) is used to instantly communicate success. (Detailed in Chapter 4)

Step 3: Reinforce immediately

Timely reinforcement is provided to support future success. (Detailed in Chapter 5)

Let's look at each side of the TAGteach Triangle in more depth.

3 TAGteach Triangle—Identify

In this chapter, we introduce:

- FOCUS FUNNEL

- TAG POINTS

- WOOF

- "THE TAG POINT IS"

- TARGETING

- PERSONALIZING THE TAG POINT

- DEMONSTRATIONS

In the space between teaching and learning, lies a sweet spot. A goal that perfectly coordinates with a student's ability and their desire to succeed.

The "Identify" side of the triangle provides unique tools to help a teacher efficiently break down, build up, tease out, and deliver the perfect goal for their learner—every time.

3.1 Focus Funnel

Imagine taking a lecture from a teacher, coach, leader, or parent, and pouring it into a funnel. Imagine the amount of information getting smaller and more instructional as the funnel narrows until a single point of success for the learner is revealed. This is the focus funnel—a tool for the teacher, that guides the creation of clear instructions and a single goal designed for immediate success. It's a tool for the learner, that assists in the transition from listening mode to action mode.

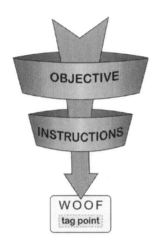

The focus funnel is created with the three foundation phrases. Each leads the student and the teacher down through the funnel, toward the final, single criterion for success.

▼ TAG—Focus Funnel

The objective is: ...

The teacher begins the transition from a larger lecture/lesson and begins to introduce a more refined objective for the learner.

The instructions are: ...

Only specific instruction(s) regarding the learner's upcoming action can make it through this narrowed point in the funnel.

The tag point is: ...

The end of the funnel is only wide enough to accommodate a single goal. It's like the teacher saying, "I don't want you to guess what is important, so I'll make it very clear. This is the most important thing to do."

This goal can only be considered a tag point when it is refined with the WOOF criteria (discussed in Section 3.3).

Here's an example of a lesson that would benefit from a trip through the focus funnel:

Basketball Coach: "Remember to bounce the ball with your fingertips. I've told you that before. Do you remember why we do that? Well, it's because you have more control that way. If you hit the ball with your palm, you have very little control and the ball can get away from you. You don't want to dribble down the court and lose control of the ball and have the other team grab it and score. So all you have to do is remember to touch the ball with just your fingertips as you are dribbling down the court. Okay, let's try it again and remember what I told you. You can do it!"

Although this is all true, it can be a lot to take in for any student. So, immediately before the coach asks the player to attempt the skill, she employs the focus funnel to reduce her virtual paragraph into a single set of instructions and sets up the most important goal as the tag point.

▼ TAG—Focus Funnel

"Okay, listen up!"

The objective is: to improve your ball control, use your fingertips to dribble the ball.

The instructions are: as you dribble from the starting line to the cone, use your fingertips to dribble the ball.

The tag point is: fingertips touch ball.

Notes:

You may notice—we leave out a lot of words. Grammar and sentence structure has to be tossed. All that remains are the words vital to the performance of the tag point (goal).

The focus funnel language may feel stilted the first few times. But the benefits take no time at all. Learners snap to attention and listen when they hear the phrase that will tell them exactly what they need to succeed—and nothing more.

3.1.1 Focus Funnel—for Server Training in Restaurants

A restaurant owner wants the service staff to add a step in the customer order process. The manager calls the staff in for a micro-training session.

Manager: "In response to an increase of incorrect orders making it to the table, the management has decided to add a step to the process of taking orders from the customers. We can't have customers receiving an incorrect order because you didn't hear or write down what they said correctly. From now on everyone needs to double-check that what you wrote down on the order ticket is actually what the customer wants. After you write down the order, repeat it back to the customer. When they confirm the order, place a check mark at the top of the order ticket. This means every order, every time. It will only take a second and should clear up any miscommunication between you and the customer. The check mark means you have 'double checked' to make sure the order is complete and correct.

"Again, after you write down the order, repeat it back to the customer. When they confirm the order, place a check mark at the top of the order ticket. The check mark means you have "checked" to make sure the order is complete and correct. Okay, let's practice this new step a few times before you try it with real customers."

▼ TAG—Focus Funnel

"Okay, let's practice this new step a few times before you try it with live customers."

The objective is: confirm orders from customers.

The instructions are: repeat customer order and ask, "Is that correct?" When the customer confirms, make a check mark on the top of the order ticket.

The tag point is: make "check mark" on ticket.

Using the focus funnel in this instance, helped the restaurant manager make a clean break from the lecture, and refocus on delivering the information the learners needed to succeed right now. He chose "check mark" as a tag point, as it was the last step in the chain of actions: repeat, ask, confirm, make a check mark.

3.1.2 Focus Funnel—for the Elementary Classroom

The principal has asked all teachers to review the "hands off" rules for lining up.

Teacher: "There have been way too many pushing and shoving incidents when we line up to go outside. Someone is going to get hurt. You remember when the principal came in and told us that she didn't want anyone pushing to get in line? She told you that whether you are the first person in line or the last person in line, you will all get to go outside. So please stop pushing as you get in line. Plus, these are not the good manners that we talked about last week. I know this class has good manners, we just need to practice them a bit more so that when the bell rings and you are excited about going outside, you can still remember to line up without putting your hands on other students. So, remember, this class knows how to use their manners. When you line up, do not touch anyone else."

▼ TAG—Focus Funnel

"All right, class, it's time to practice lining up."

The objective is: line up with good manners.

The instructions are: when your row is asked to line up, get up from your chair, push it under the table, then put your hands on your hips.

The tag point is: hands on hips.

Using the focus funnel, helped the teacher organize her thoughts and present a single objective, instruction and a unique goal that will encourage the learners to keep their hands off others, "hands on hips."

3.1.3   TAGteach Tale: Focus Funnel Technique Benefits Teachers and Students

Kate Jackson, Classroom Teacher
East Anglia, UK

I'm a teacher, and I am on the autism spectrum. I'm both high and low functioning but have achieved a level of integration in "normal" society because of my higher functioning attributes. It has been a difficult path to walk alone. Sometimes I still find it difficult to communicate clearly and effectively, even on relatively high-functioning days.

Now that I use TAGteach tools, they have dramatically improved my ability to relay new information to my students, while increasing their ability to follow instructions. When I write instructions for my students' homework, I do it using a focus funnel. The funnel makes it easier to read and understand, and easier for me to use as a teacher/coach. There was immediate and measurable success with this method in my classrooms.

The tools have revolutionized my teaching style and confidence. I wish I'd known how to do this when I was a child—my life would have been less stressful and everyday tasks less confusing to perform and master.

3.2 Tag Points Are the "Point" of Success

Remember when we said TAGteach is a methodology to bring a teacher and a learner together at the moment of learning? Well, the tag point is that moment. We introduced the tag point as the end product of the focus funnel—but a tag point has a life all of its own.

A tag point is designed to be, when accomplished, the actual point of success. The very instant when a teacher can say without reservation, "Yes, that goal was performed to perfection." For those haunted by the voice of a past coach reminding them that, "nothing is ever perfect," a successful tag point by definition is perfection and sweet vindication.

So, how do we create tag points? Just remember the acronym WOOF.

3.3 WOOF—It's What You Want

To create the perfect tag point, you may have to change your perspective. That's because teachers, coaches, leaders and even parents have been conditioned to identify what the learner is doing wrong and then tell them to stop.

Tag points are first and foremost what you want them "to do."

WOOF

W = What you want

Identify what it is you want the learner *to do*.

O = One thing

A TAGteach goal has a single point of success so that it can be quickly and cleanly tagged (identified) when achieved.

O = Observable

The answer to the learner's question, "Did it happen?" must be observable to an outsider.

F = Five words or fewer

Stick to a bare-bones description for what you're trying to achieve, one that's easy to remember as the student attempts the action. Five words or fewer is the rule.

Using WOOF criteria ensures the tag point is a goal that can be understood by the learner and with a reasonable amount of effort, performed to perfection.

For example:

A horseback riding instructor learns his student is not yet comfortable feeding treats to her schooling horse. The instructor decides to use TAGteach and starts with a short lecture and then transitions into the focus funnel.

Instructor: "You told me that you are afraid to feed the horse. Well, that is understandable, and you should never feed a horse you don't know. But your schooling horse today is Smokey, and he has been taught to be very gentle when taking his treats. If you want, I can show you a safe way to deliver his treats. Yes? That's great. We can practice with each other first, and then if you feel comfortable, we can try feeding Smokey. Would you like to try it with me? Great! Let's play the tag game."

▼ TAG—Focus Funnel

The objective is: to safely feed Smokey.

The instructions are: with all your fingers and thumbs touching, hold your hand flat.

The tag point is: flat hand.

> W: I want the learner to keep a flat hand when feeding Smokey.
>
> O: "Flat hand" has a single criterion.
>
> O: "Flat hand" is observable.
>
> F: "Flat hand" has five words or fewer.

3.3.1 Tag Points—for a Successful Preschool Dance Class

Dance Teacher: "Okay, dancers, your parents will be joining us at the end of class to see what you learned today. I think we should show them how you walk across the dance floor. Who remembers how dancers walk? That's right! We stretch our feet. We practiced this last week, but we can practice again today. I think your parents will be very impressed."

▼ TAG—Focus Funnel

The objective is: stretch your feet when walking across the dance floor.

The instructions are: walk across the dance floor, and before each step, stretch your foot.

The tag point is: stretch foot.

> W: I want the dancer to stretch her foot.
>
> O: "Stretch foot" has a single criterion.
>
> O: "Stretch foot" is observable.

F: "Stretch foot" has five words or fewer.

3.3.2 Tag Points—for Basketball Players

Instructor: "Okay, we want to practice shooting. Start by creating a good base by putting the dominant foot just a couple of inches in front of the other foot, about shoulder width apart, toes pointing at the basket, and knees bent. The farther away from the basket you are, the more you bend your knees. Back straight, chest up, dominant hand under the ball with wrist fully flexed and arm at a ninety-degree angle. Non-dominant arm supports ball. Shoot straight up as you jump up, and end with your elbow above your eyebrow."

*As you can see, shooting a basketball requires many individual skills and physical adjustments that all happen concurrently. You can create a series of tag points and build the technique of shooting until the skill is mastered—point toes toward the basket, bend knees, chest out, wrist flexed fully, shoot straight up, end with elbow above eyebrow. The first skill often taught to young kids is the importance of using your legs and aiming your feet at the basket.

▼ TAG—Focus Funnel

The objective is: to line your body up with the basket before you shoot.

The instructions are: line up shot with toes toward basket.

The tag point is: point toes toward basket.

> W: I want the athletes to line up shot with toes toward the basket.
>
> O: "Point toes toward basket" is a single criterion.
>
> O: "Point toes toward basket" is observable.
>
> F: "Point toes toward basket" is five words or fewer.

3.3.3 TAGteach Tale: Physical Therapy and Tag Points at Home

Lynette Cole
Los Angeles, California

In October of 2011, my husband had brain surgery. This was not his first, but it was his most difficult. Because of balance issues before surgery, a physical therapist was sent to evaluate and work with him after the operation. Everything seemed to be good, except for his dragging the toes on his right foot.

The therapist and I were walking him around the hospital floor. She had to keep reminding him over and over to lift the toes on his right foot (so they would not drag). About halfway through the session, it hit me that I could fix this.

I told the therapist I'd be right back. I retrieved my clicker from my purse and caught up with them. My husband and I had talked about TAGteach before, so I just told him, "**The tag point is:** toes up."

The physical therapist looked at me a little funny, so I told her my husband understood what I meant, and I repeated, "Toes up." As we started the trip back to his room, I tagged each time he lifted his toes to step with, "Toes up." He immediately began lifting his toes without being reminded. The tag point gave him one thing to focus on, and it worked.

When we returned to his room, I explained tag points and the audible mark to his physical therapist. The next day, the three of us did the walk again. This time I only had to say the tag point once and tag about three times as we got close to his room. That was the end of the toe-dragging problem. We could not be happier with the outcome.

3.4 Delivering the Tag Point—the Tag Point Is

Tag points keep bad things from happening to good information with these guidelines:

- Minimal wording: **"The tag point is"** is a convenient transition for those of us who ramble our way around instructions and try to get back to exactly what we want the learner to do.

- Calming: **"The tag point is"** has a calming effect on anxious learners when used consistently. Learners know the phrase means the teacher has taken the time to refine the goal and that they are very likely to succeed.

- Attention-grabbing: **"The tag point is"** becomes a call to—and for—attention. "Hey, an opportunity for positive reinforcement is coming."

- Maintains objective phrasing: **"The tag point is"** keeps the focus on an action instead of a person. This may help reduce social distractions, like the fear of being judged harshly or displeasing the teacher.

- Eliminates "I" and "you": **"The tag point is"** eliminates the need for the words I, you, we, and their—derivatives that may carry a hint of bribery.

Examples:

I want you to put your hands in your pockets.

The tag point is: hands in pockets.

(Eliminated you, your, and you'll)

I want you to keep your leg straight.

The tag point is: leg straight.

(Eliminated I, you, and your)

If you start your letter at the top, you'll get a tag.

The tag point is: start at the top.

(Eliminated you, your, and you'll)

3.5 Target Tag Points—a Bullseye on Success

While having a simple tag point for certain activities is effective, such as with dribbling a basketball—"fingers touch ball"—learning other skills requires a more targeted method. In the examples below, TAGteach uses "tag points" with targets to achieve success.

- Targets may be naturally available in the environment or artificially created by the teacher.

- Targets are always clearly recognizable to the learner and the teacher.

3.5.1 Target Tag Points—for the Orthopaedic Surgical Resident

An orthopaedic surgical resident habitually raises his elbows when he practices drilling "bone" on a PVC pipe. The instructor knows there is more stability if the elbows are kept close to the body, but the process of spreading out the arms is involuntary, like a batter getting ready to swing—something everyone has done or seen. The instructor creates a tag point with a physical target to highlight the new position.

The focus funnel, in this case, helped the instructor whittle down the information being relayed to the surgical resident.

▼ TAG—Focus Funnel

The objective is: to keep your elbows close to your body to create more stability when drilling into a bone.

The instructions are: before engaging the drill, brace elbows against your ribs.

The tag point is: elbows to rib (ribs are naturally available). Or—

The tag point is: elbows to tape (place blue tape on the learner's ribs). Or—

The tag point is: tape to tape (place blue tape on elbows and ribs). Or—

The tag point is: blue to blue (same as above).

3.5.2 Target Tag Points—for Physical Therapy

Jeff's physical therapy patient, a local tennis instructor, is regaining strength after an injury. He wants to make sure the tennis player lifts his leg to the right height to activate the recovering muscles. Jeff has put a piece of tape on the wall to create a clear point of reference or "target" for his client.

▼ TAG—Focus Funnel

The objective is: to perform the exercise with a proper range of motion.

The instructions are: tighten the leg muscles and then lift the leg to the height of the tape on the wall.

The tag point is: leg to tape.

3.5.3 Target Tag Points—to Maintain Preschool Manners

The preschool teacher has taped smiley-face stickers under each student's table, which correspond to where the chair legs should be when the chair is properly pushed in.

▼ TAG—Focus Funnel

The objective is: leave your work area neat and safe.

The instructions are: before you leave, push the chair under the table.

The tag point is: chair legs to smiley faces.

3.5.4 TAGteach Tale: Learning to Play the Cello

Robin and Tayja Jhane Sallie
Boston, Massachusetts

My daughter, Tayja, and I have used TAGteach for years with things like schoolwork, sports, and cello practice. Using the marker instead of my "mommy" voice has kept any attitudes and judgments from creeping in and altering the mood or ruining the practice session altogether.

For cello practices, we preferred using a box clicker to tag while Tayja was playing, so that it could be heard above the sound of the cello. Here are a few tag points that worked for us:

▼ TAG—Focus Funnel

The objective is: have proper posture to improve sound quality.

The instructions are: before you bring the bow to the position, place your feet on the targets.

The tag point is: feet on targets.

In another exercise—

In order to make taking the notes from the page to the instrument more fluid, I used color-coded targets (sticky stars) to match the notes on the strings to the notes on the page.

▼ TAG—Focus Funnel

The objective is: to play more fluidly by memorizing the notes that are being played.

The instructions are: match the colored stars on the page with the colored stars on the instrument

The tag point is: fingers touch target.

The targets made the desirable behavior clear, easy, and they did the reinforcing, over mom doing the "nagging." By the time the sticky stars fell off, she didn't need them anymore.

3.5.5 TAGteach Tale: Target Tag Points and Pro Golf Create a Perfect Swing

Cheryl Anderson
2006 National LPGA Teacher of the Year
2010 *Golf Digest*, "Top 15 Women in America"

Players can be so focused on where the ball is going, they overlook the skills needed to get the ball there. With tag points, I designed incremental goals and, more importantly, mini-achievements for a sport in which the ultimate goal of a perfect swing may never happen.

▼ TAG—Focus Funnel

The objective is: elbows stay close to your body when the club head meets the ball. This will keep the club face in the right place at the beginning and end of swing.

The instructions are: as you swing the club back down, brush your elbows to your pocket.

The tag point is: elbows to pocket.

Tag points have changed the way I teach—and will teach—for the rest of my career. I like that I don't have to correct my students every time. The students are self-correcting because they either hear the tag or they don't, which is where the true learning happens.

3.6 Personalized Tag Points—I'll Do It Myself

Sometimes the learner knows best. If you're not sure what the tag point should be, just ask the learner!

Here are two scenarios where the learner defines the tag point:

3.6.1 Personalized Tag Point—Tennis

Coach: "The tennis racket should be in 'this' position at the end of the follow-through. What do you want to call that?"

Athlete: "It feels like the racket is brushing by my ear in that position."

Coach: "Great!"

 TAG—Focus Funnel

The objective is: to improve the follow through position.

(*as the coach and athlete were already discussing it, the coach may decide not to verbalize "the objective is.")

The instructions are: complete the swing with the racket to "brush ear."

The tag point is: brush ear.

3.6.2 Personalized Tag Point—Gymnastics

Coach: "Put your arms straight out to the side—right about here." (Coach places the gymnast's arms in a very specific position.) "What do you want to call that exact place?"

Gymnast: "Um, airplane arms!"

Coach: "Okay!"

TAG—Focus Funnel

The objective is: to have the arms in the correct position.

(*as the coach and athlete were already discussing it, the coach may decide not to repeat the objective.)

The instructions are: when you land the leap on the beam, go to airplane arms.

The tag point is: airplane arms.

3.6.3 TAGteach Tale: Successfully Instructing Chatty Seven-Year-Old Dancers

Beth Wheeler
TAGteach Cofounder
Owner, A Dancer's Dream studio
Marblehead, MA

Scenario: I had a class of six tap students (all under the age of seven) who lost focus and started talking to each other. Instead of insisting that they stop talking and pay attention, I delivered a tag point.

"**The tag point is:** sit on floor."

I caught each dancer as they plopped to the floor. "Click, click, click, click, click, click." Instead of being scolded for a momentary lapse of attention, they had completed a task! Each was excited to have earned a tag and had their eyes locked on me. Win-win!

Note: Beth decided the full focus funnel was not necessary nor expedient in this situation.

3.6.4 TAGteach Tale: Training Zookeepers to Train Exotic Big Cats

Theresa Mckeon, TAGteach International
Laura Monaco Torelli, KPA CTP, CPDT-KA, CPBC
Chicago, Illinois

Theresa: "When Laura Monaco Torelli asked me to present a TAGteach workshop to the animal keepers at Niabi Zoo, I was thrilled. Laura and I had worked together on several occasions when both people and animals needed training, and we agreed, nagging doesn't work on cougars any more than it works on people.

Laura, a professional animal trainer, had been teaching the staff at Niabi about clicker training and how optimal learning occurs when information is delivered in finite bits, immediately marked, and then followed up with reinforcement. She wanted the keepers to experience how these principles hold true for any learner—including people—and suggested they learn about TAGteach.

Laura explained to the zookeepers how TAGteach could be used to break down and train the complex skills they needed in order to handle, train, and reinforce the big cats (lion, tigers, cougars, leopards, jaguar, and bobcats) safely and efficiently.

The group seemed on board and we started the training with one particular skill that was more complicated than it appeared— delivering reinforcement to the animal during training. It's actually a long chain of skills the keepers must perform: observing, cueing, clicking, measuring, and gathering chopped meat from a bucket attached to their belt, attaching and delivering the meat with tongs or feed poles (to keep the keepers' hands safe), and resetting. In mere seconds these tasks must be performed and with little-to-no extraneous physical movement.

Laura and I used the focus funnel and developed a training plan for our human learners. Several tag points were derived from our efforts, but one became the keepers' favorite.

The lecture: "The feed pole that delivers the meat must be removed from the cat's view immediately after feeding. If the pole stays in clear view, the lion may visually follow it (waiting for more food to appear) instead of looking back to the trainer for the next cue."

*Instead of constantly reminding them of what not to do "Don't wave that pole around!" the group landed on an acceptable, neutral position to place the pole: side of body; touching pant leg; pointing downward. The group named the position "home".

▼ TAG—Focus Funnel

The objective is: return the feed pole to a neutral position that doesn't draw the cat's focus.

The instructions are: after delivery, immediately move the feed pole to home position.

The tag point is: initiate pole to home.

After just a few rounds of practice with the tag points, the keepers consistently moved the feed pole to the home position.

Colleen, the head keeper at Niabi at the time, was kind enough to send us her thoughts after the training.

"To enhance and expand the communication skills of our staff, we were introduced to the principles of TAGteach. Using the TAGteach concepts, we were able to clearly set criteria and offer positive feedback to each other. We can all benefit from this type of teaching, which focuses on what is correct rather than the opposite."

—Colleen Stalf, Head Keeper
Niabi Zoological Park.

4 TAGteach Triangle—Tag

In this chapter, we introduce:

- THE TAG
- TAG TIMING
- OFF-POINT ERRORS
- TAGGING ON THE FLY

You have "identified" the goal and delivered information to your learner with absolute precision. Now you can deliver instant feedback with equal precision: the Tag.

A golf instructor once told me, "If I had my way, students wouldn't practice their swing with a golf ball until they had solid swing mechanics." She explained, "Students, especially adults, judge their success by where the ball lands and so often they are disappointed. I tell them over and over again to focus on their mechanics. Focus on improving the placement of your hips, or elbows, or your follow through—not the ball. It's a losing battle." I asked her, "Can't you just take the ball away?" She shook her head and sighed, "I've tried. But clients don't like it, and they'll find another instructor."

This is the seriousness of timely feedback. Students who put forth effort want to know if they succeed and, more importantly, want to know *when* they succeed. Feedback that is delivered late or with wishy-washy information can derail the learners' attempts to make corrections or remember what they did right going forward.

TAGteach feedback comes in the form of an audible mark or tag—placed at the exact moment of success.

4.1 The Tag—Second Side of the TAGteach Triangle

Whether audible, visual, or tactile, the tag is always:

- **Brief:**

  Marks the instant an action occurs—

  > "Yes, that thing you are doing right now is correct."

- **Binary:**

  Because the tag point has been carefully crafted into a format where success has a yes or no answer, the feedback is clear and binary.

  o Tag = action happening.

  o No tag = not currently happening.

- **Informative:**

  Feedback the learner can use.

  o If the goal was met (as demonstrated with a tag), the student makes a mental note to do it again "that way."

  o If the goal was not met, (no tag is heard, seen, or felt) the student self-assesses, tries again, or asks for help.

- **Positive:**

The tag always says, "Yes."

As with anything that always brings good news, the tag quickly becomes sought after. Learners want to make it happen again. Now the tag has the potential to become positive reinforcement.

4.1.1 Tag—Tag Points and Off-Point Errors

If the tag point criterion is performed, that attempt is 100% successful.

Errors unrelated to the tag point are called off-point errors. These are momentarily shelved (mentally or detailed in notes). They can be discussed at another time and/or turned into additional tag points.

Example:

Gymnastic coach delivers a focus funnel.

▼ TAG—Focus Funnel

The objective is: to point toes when doing a handstand.

The instructions are: do a handstand and hold for five seconds.

The tag point is: point toes.

*Coach uses a plastic clicker to audibly tag the action "point toes."

The gymnast kicks up into a handstand and points her toes but has bent arms. The coach must adhere to the tag point as the complete point of success. The coach tags the moment the gymnast's toes point with his clicker. The coach then notes: *After a few more tags for pointed toes, I'll address the bent elbow error.*

4.1.2 The Clicker—You Win!

Although the tag stimulus can be made in many different ways, we started with a small, mechanical box clicker. The click sound cut through the ambient noise in the gymnasium, it didn't have any other meaning to the athletes, was easy to carry, and the click was as fast as the blink of an eye.

Because it was only paired with success, the sound of the clicker was something the athletes quickly learned to love. A young volleyball player told us: *"It's like a game, and the click tells you when you win."*

If the sound of the mechanical tag is inappropriate in a particular situation (competition, silent learning environments, etc.), a visual or tactile marker can be used.

But don't be afraid to give a clicker or a similar single-sound marker a try. The electronic world has known about the power of the "click" for a long time.

- A reviewer describes a particular keyboard as *"...Extremely popular [because it] offers that audible, tactile 'click.'"* He goes on to say, *"The audible key-clicks and the sure knowledge every time you press down on a key that it's registered properly is a feeling you really have to experience to appreciate. Plus, that audible and tactile feedback can improve your game or help you minimize typos, especially if you type quickly."*[5]

- Launch Sound is a Smartphone app that provides a "click" sound when an app has been launched.[6]

- The Perfect Situp®, a patented exercise machine, assists in workouts by providing a "click" when an ab crunch is done properly. *"Hear that click? That's the sound of*

[5] http://alturl.com/9q8xe

[6] https://youtu.be/sa6hCWBje3s

success. This audible coach locks you on target. No wasted effort."[7]

4.1.3 TAGteach Tale: A Clicker Simplifies the Autism/Parenting Challenge

Martha Gabler, parent and author
Chaos to Calm:
Discovering Solutions to the Everyday Problems of Living with Autism

TAGteach blasts through the liabilities because the sound indicates success to the child, and success is great! We all like success, and kids with autism generally experience very little success.

Despite the sensory issues and the language processing issues, the click rings loud and clear and tells the child that he or she did something right. Once the child realizes that his or her own action results in helpful information and reinforcement, he or she looks for more opportunities to get more of these good things. From that point on, it is just a matter of observing the child, noting which actions are helpful or positive, then tagging and reinforcing those actions. When a child is successfully learning functional behaviors, and they are able to participate in more pleasant activities, horizons expand and difficult and angry behavioral attitudes and outbursts may decline.

4.1.4 Verbal Tag

If you choose to use a word or verbal sound, there are a few rules.

Use a word or sound that has as little emotional baggage as possible.

    a.   Many people use the word "tag" instead of a click.

    b.   A quick "yep" works, too.

Although it is not the best choice, if you must use common words like "yes" or "good", try to say them in a neutral manner, and with as little

---

[7] http://alturl.com/rfb5m

passion as possible. The perceived cheerleading that is often attached to those words can be distracting as the learner asks, "Was it good, good*ish* or was it perfect?"

4.2 Tag Timing

The most effective tag highlights the action right as it occurs. This eliminates confusion.

If the tag point is "stand on one leg," a perfect tag would come the millisecond the leg begins to leave the ground. Now the tag is contributing to the learner's confidence, as well as delivering information.

If you accidentally tag but the action did not occur, just say so! "Whoops, I shouldn't have tagged that." (Because my gymnasts "collected" their tags to use in the TAG store, if I tagged something by mistake, they would still get to keep that tag for their "bank.")

If a student becomes annoyed with the sound of the tag, reevaluate your timing. A late tag leaves the learner struggling for a decision: "Did I do it or not?"

4.3 Tag—the Benefits

4.3.1 Tag—Faster Than a Speeding Bullet

The tag is swift by design—especially with mechanical devices like clickers, where the information travels quickly and cuts through the ambient noise in the learning environment.

Some wonder whether it's possible to have multiple tag sessions happening simultaneously within the same limited space, such as a classroom. Don't all the tags flying around create confusion?

As it turns out, students are surprisingly good at determining if a tag is meant for them. Timing and physical orientation all play a part. If an inconsistent tag hits their radar it is quickly disregarded. If confusion does arise, students can take turns, use a different marker, or find a more accommodating space.

4.3.2 Tag—Skips the "Better/But"

Few things can sabotage learning like the phrase, "That was better." It's unclear. "In what way was it better?" It's also typically the prelude to, "But next time..." The yes/no design of the tag points and the clear feedback does away with that option. The tag point was either a success, or it wasn't.

4.3.3 Tag—a Working Pause

Using a tag creates a momentary space without verbal communication from the teacher. The learner can opt to stay in the learning bubble and process information.

Learner: *I heard the tag. This is correct. Remember this.*

These extra seconds in silence may help learners problem-solve when they go solo.

4.3.4 Tag—Please, but No Thank You

What would you do if your instructor yelled, "Good job!" when you performed your skill? Many of us would feel the need to respond with, "Thank you!"

This social response may show respect, but it's not always desirable if the learner is engaged in an activity that requires intense focus, or that may involve physical danger (e.g., a gymnast flipping in the air).

The tag has no history with, or need for, social responses. It's just information.

4.3.5 Tag—Separates Information from Praise

Even when encouragement is the intent, verbal remarks may come across as insincere and condescending.

The tag is pure information: "Yes, what you are doing is correct."

Example:

Therapist: "Okay, Mr. Conroy, let's do arm raises. I need you to do the exercise ten times and really concentrate on raising the arms above a level that's horizontal to the ground. I noticed during your last visit, you were getting to horizontal a few times, but most times you were shy of horizontal. It's to be expected, as I'm sure you're getting tired, but let's try to push hard today. You can do it."

"Okay, go ahead and start and do ten horizontal arm raises."

Mr. Conroy raises his arms.

"Good job."

"Thanks," he says and does it again.

"Good, keep going."

He does it a third time.

"Oops. See, that time you didn't make it all the way."

"Sorry about that," He tries again.

"That's better."

Mr. Conroy raises his arms for the fifth time.

"Yep."

He does it again.

"A little more next time."

"Right, sorry." He tries again.

"Even a little more."

He struggles this time.

"Come on, you're almost there."

He goes again.

"Higher, higher, higher."

Mr. Conroy groans.

"Pretty good for last one. That's always the tough one."

"Thanks."

"Okay, great job—much better. Let's move on to the next exercise."

In the physical therapy example above, the therapist's verbal feedback is doing triple duty as: "yes/no" information, a "do it again" prompt, and even a bit of cheerleading. The learner will try to tease out the important information while focusing on performing the exercise, which creates feedback that is misleading, frustrating, and exhausting.

In contrast, using the tag (a click, a thumbs-up, or a neutrally delivered "yes"), removes the need for a social response until the exercise is over. The therapist is then free to praise the patient's performance, effort, and/or positive attitude.

Let's try this scenario again using a TAGteach focus funnel and an audible tag (click).

The therapist places a piece of blue painters' tape on the wall to create a visual target for Mr. Conroy. Now, the exact height (the criterion for success) is no longer subjective but a single point, which is clear to both of them.

▼ TAG—Focus Funnel

The objective is: improve strength and range of motion of the injured shoulder.

The instructions are: lift arm to "this mark" on the wall for ten repetitions.

The tag point is: lift arm to mark.

(The therapist uses a metal clicker to audibly tag the action—"arm to mark.")

After delivering all the necessary information via the focus funnel, the therapist is quiet as Mr. Conroy begins the exercise for ten repetitions. The client is free to focus on executing the tag point and processing the feedback:

Tag = "yes"

No tag = "try again"

1. Arm reaches tape = click

2. Arm reaches tape = click

3. Arm reaches tape = click

4. Arm stops two inches below tape = no click

5. Patient refocuses and lifts his arm to tape = click

6. Arm reaches tape = click

7. Arm reaches tape = click

8. Arm reaches tape = click

9. Patient is getting tired and stops below tape = no click

10. Patient takes a breath and gives extra effort to reach the tape = click

When the client finishes the set, the therapist offers praise and support of the effort. "Well done, Mr. Conroy. Your strength is improving, and you really dug deep for that last one. Rest a minute and then we'll move on to the next exercise."

4.3.6 Tag—the End of the Praise Junkie

Praise in the right amount is wonderful. Many of us are motivated by sincere, specific recognition from those we respect. But endless verbal praise may also encourage us to become a "praise junkie."[8] The drawback? Praise junkies find verbal praise more reinforcing than the stress involved in achieving the skill. The goal of a praise junkie is to receive the praise (not perfect the skill).

Using a tag to indicate success may help reduce the conditions that create and maintain the learner's desire for constant and immediate verbal praise. The tag point establishes clear criteria for success. The tag sound (or signal) is neutral and does not convey emotion or social approval.

Since the tag typically takes on a reinforcing property, due to its consistent pairing with success, the student works for success, not praise from the teacher. The tag just means "yes, that was right." The absence of the tag directs the learner to self-assess, try again, or ask for help. Independent thought and self-motivation are pushed to the forefront as the learning process is now in the hands of the learner.

4.3.7 Tag—for Documenting Success

Tags are like little bits of documented success. One young dancer ran to her mother after class, yelling, "Mommy, I got thirty-eight tags!"

Tags can be counted, documented, and turned into tokens (which I have explored and will expand on further below). The tags can also be logged as data for grant writing, staff reviews, and personnel assessment.

4.3.8 Tag—the Neutral Third Party

Children may be intimidated by teachers, and adults often fear failure in the presence of other adults.

---

[8] http://www.urbandictionary.com/define.php?term=Praise+junkie

When a tag is used, information feels like it's coming from a neutral third party. A moment has been created where a learner can focus on performing a skill, instead of performing for the teacher.

4.3.9 Tag—Can't You Just Say, "Good Job?"

You can use your words to tag success, but there are trade-offs.

"Good" doesn't always mean good.

Thomas wonders, *Coach Larry practically screamed, "Yes!" the first time I hit the ball. But this time it was just kind of an ordinary, "Yes." I wonder if I did something wrong, or if the coach is just distracted?*

Human language is, by design, packed with physical and emotional nuances, which take time and focus to process. The tag sound doesn't fluctuate in response to human emotion. It just means "yes."

"When the teachers tell you, 'Good,' you don't really think about it. But when you hear the tag, you take a mental picture of yourself in that position and you know to go to that position the next time."

—Henry, twelve-year-old dancer
Boston, MA

4.4 Tag—Tagging on the Fly

Tag points can be created and included in your curriculum and lesson plans.

However, teaching opportunities can happen unexpectedly. In these instances, with TAGteach, you can quickly establish order and clarity using a focus funnel to create a few tag points. We call this "tagging on the fly."

4.4.1 TAGteach Tale: Tagging on the Fly—Corporate Training, Advanced DISC

Glenn Hughes, Director of Global Learning Architecture, KLA-Tencor:
Training magazine "Top 10 Hall of Fame" company

I contacted Ed Muzio, author of Four Secrets to Liking Your Work: You May Not Need to Quit to Get the Job You Want, to certify my team of eight people in Advanced DISC, which is a behavioral assessment tool much like Meyers-Briggs.

On day one, Ed noted that we were going to be a challenging group. We all possessed between three and ten years of DISC training experience. Our language patterns were well established. We were used to phrases like "She's a D," or "He's an I," or "I'm a D."

In Advanced DISC, it is very important to steer away from labels and move to observations of behavioral patterns. Ed wanted us to use phrases like, "You show high D behavior," or "She shows low I behavior," or "He shows high S behavior." Despite his pleading, begging, modeling the correct behavior, and calling out our misuse of the language, we didn't change our behavior.

On the morning of day two, Ed and I were chatting about different learning events we'd been doing, and I shared my TAGteach experience. Ed asked, "Could we use it on our problem?"

My response was, "Hmm. I hadn't thought about using it to change language or culture, but it's an observable behavior, so yes. I think we can."

On day two, we implemented TAGteach.

Since everyone in the room was a facilitator, I opened the morning by teaching them the history and process of TAGteach.

We identified the target behavior and created the focus funnel.

TAG—Focus Funnel

The objective is: use correct behavioral language.

The instructions are: use the phrase, "High/low 'X' behavior."

The tag point is: say, "Behavior."

*We did not have a clicker, so we had to improvise. We agreed that a finger snap would be the tag.

Ed then spent fifteen minutes modeling correct and incorrect behavior, so we could practice tagging.

Ed spent the rest of the morning (2.5 hours) teaching us Advanced DISC. Every time the tag point was performed, we tagged with a snap.

In the afternoon, each facilitator led a teach-back for our certification. During these three hours, the audience was reinforcing the targeted phrase with claps/snaps.

Result: In one day, we re-patterned the language (behavior) of eight facilitators. In the debriefing with Ed the next day, he commented that our success rate of using the correct phrase on day one was 0%. By the end of day two (facilitator teach-backs), he estimated that we had over a 70% success rate. He felt that we would not have improved more than 10% without applying TAGteach. Additionally, we saw a number of classic effects. Two of them were increased energy—everyone had fun with it, as opposed to being annoyed by corrections, and, self-correction—by mid-morning, people would sense that they were not "tagged" and correct their language.

Self-learning: One facilitator missed the morning history, process, and tag point identification. In the afternoon, after her teach-back, I asked if she knew why we were snapping all day. She responded, "Of course. You're reinforcing the use of the correct phrase."

Obviously, we were thrilled with this outcome and could see many more applications. I'll definitely run more on-site certification sessions for my colleagues in the near future.

4.4.2 TAGteach Tale: Tagging on the Fly—a Stuffy Nose

Keri Gorman, Senior TAGteach Instructor and Mother

Portland, OR

After having spent five years teaching TAGteach to others, I finally came across a potentially difficult situation with my three-year-old son, Max. Well, actually, I was in the middle of the difficult situation when my husband said to me, "Why don't you try tagging instead? I'll get the video camera."

This event occurred during that two-to-three-year-old timeframe in which kids are perpetually sick and the snot just keeps coming. The only real relief I could offer my son was a shot of saline up the nose, which is not a pleasant experience to most toddlers, and Max was no exception. He kept running away from me, screaming.

Max and I had already played around with tag points here and there. I had taught him some sign language, how to kick a ball, and how to wash his hair using the TAGteach system, so he had experience with tagging as a fun game.

Yet, for some reason, I was hesitant to use it when things were really falling apart. Maybe I was afraid to poison it—take away its elements of fun and connection. My husband had a point, though. Isn't this exactly what TAGteach is for?

In our TAGteach seminars, we emphasize having a teaching plan, breaking skills down, and being organized in our sessions. Unfortunately, parenthood doesn't quite work that way. I was truly "tagging on the fly."

I started by putting the clicker in Max's hand. I didn't have any reinforcers other than my enthusiasm, and to give him control and a reprieve from being the learner—or in this case, the patient.

The opportunity to tag me as soon as I squirted the saline up his nose turned out to be reinforcing for Max. Of course, the highlight of the session came when Max figured out he could squirt me with the bottle. Now, we were really having fun while continuing to get the task done. It was a huge relief—to both of us—when Max was finally able to let me apply the nose spray without screaming or running for cover.

I give credit to my husband for seeing a TAGteach opportunity where I couldn't.

Check out Keri's video of Tagging on the fly: http://alturl.com/stjto

5 TAGteach Triangle—Reinforce

In this chapter, we introduce:

- POSITIVE REINFORCEMENT

- SUCCESS AS A REINFORCER

- TAGULATORS

- TOKENS

- TIERED REINFORCEMENT ARRANGEMENT

A tag point has been identified, and because it was performed, it was tagged. Two sides of the TAGteach triangle have been completed: Identify and Tag. Let's take a deeper look at positive reinforcement, the final step in the TAGteach methodology and the third side of the triangle: Reinforce.

5.1 Positive Reinforcement

Have you ever praised a learner for completing a task? Why did you praise them? Did you assume your praise was valuable to the learner and would encourage them to complete that task again in the future?

If you were right, and they did complete the task in the future, then your praise was a positive reinforcer.

Reinforcement is the process of increasing behavior with consequences. A consequence is only a reinforcer if it increases the likelihood of the learner repeating the action. Each student decides for him or herself what consequence is reinforcing. If the frequency of the behavior does not increase, then the consequence provided by the teacher was not a reinforcer for that individual. This is important information for the teacher. "The consequence I provided was not actually reinforcing for that learner's behavior."

5.1.1 Reinforce—the Sound is Positively Reinforcing

Because the tag is used exclusively to mark success, and success is typically reinforcing to a learner who wants to succeed, the tag sound itself becomes a reinforcer. It will be the desired consequence of an action.

The audible tag is an excellent reinforcer because it does not interrupt the action. It can be delivered as the behavior is happening, precisely marking the action you want the learner to repeat.

5.1.2 Reinforce—"The Tag Point Is…"

Interestingly, the use of the phrase, "The tag point is" may in itself, become reinforcing for many students. An opportunity for success that is clearly defined, and within reach, increases the likelihood that the student will attempt the action.

5.1.3 TAGteach Tale: Reinforce—Improving Your Posture

Bethan Mair Williams
Specialist Speech and Language Therapist
Board Certified Behaviour Analyst
Bangor, Wales, UK

After attending a TAGteach presentation at a conference for the Association for Behaviour Analysis International, I went back to my hotel room and told my roommate, Lisa, about the techniques. She said straight away, "That would work for me! Let's see if it can help me with my posture. My husband is always yelling at me for slouching, and I hate when he does that. It causes so many arguments."

Lisa and I looked at what she should do instead of slouch. We made "sit up straight" more observable by creating:

The tag point is: back touch chair.

If her back touched the back of the chair, she couldn't slump.

That night, in a whirl of social activity and margaritas, we had such fun, with me tagging every time I saw her "back touch chair." She was so delighted. "It's so easy! I get to know when I do it right!" "Getting it right" was reinforcing. She wanted to "get it right" again and again.

The next day, I got on the plane home and started on my plan to introduce it to my own family and the seven special schools I worked for at the time. I've been using and telling people about TAGteach ever since, including supervising students researching the techniques.

5.1.4 TAGteach Tale: Reinforce—"Because I Win!"

Victoria Fogel, BCBA, Researcher
Grand Valley State University
Allendale, Michigan

Traditionally, we have used error corrections to extinguish the incorrect behavior/skill and teach the correct behavior/skill in our behavior research program, but error corrections often appear to have the effect of punishment. They are a "This is what you did wrong" approach to learning. TAGteach does not punish the child's attempt to learn a new behavior/skill. Instead, the method reinforces the child's attempt by setting the stage for success.

For example, we used TAGteach with a child having difficulty focusing on vocalizing while counting.

The tag point was, "Say the number aloud," while he was dropping tokens into a cup. Each time he said a number, there was a tag. This provided a small success at each step and encouraged him to continue to "Say the number aloud."

I have implemented TAGteach with children diagnosed with autism and have experienced wonderful results. I have been able to fine-tune my teaching skills. Learners appear to enjoy the teaching sessions. When I asked this child why he liked the tag, he said, "Because I win!" He sure did win. He made it to twenty-seven!

5.1.5 TAGteach Tale: Reinforce—Early ABA Intervention

Brenda Terzich, MA
Founder, Applied Behavior Consultants, Inc.

Using TAGteach allows us to be "language-free" with our reinforcement. This is a tremendous benefit since many of our students have communicative deficits. Once paired with a reinforcer, the "click" is universal. Preliminary research at ABC, Inc. has shown promising results using TAGteach for a positive behavior change. TAGteach is not just for competitive athletes and gymnasts; it can be proven functional and invaluable for children with autism.

5.2 Tagulator—Tracking Success

Keeping track of success can also be very reinforcing. A tagulator is a specially designed string of beads made so that you can slide one bead (equal to one tag) down at a time. The beads can be used to keep track of tags or to mark the accomplishment.

Also called golf stroke counters or bead counters, you can buy one on Etsy or make your own.

https://www.youtube.com/watch?v=79Ao3nAmmMU

A tagulator can be placed in the car, hung on the ballet barre or a coat rack, suspended from a belt loop or backpack, or set in a specific location, such as the bathroom towel rack or any hook around the house.

▼ TAG—Focus Funnel—tagulator on towel rack

The objective is: towels need to be hung on the towel rack in order to dry properly.

The instructions are: after you finish with the towel, hang it on the rack.

The tag point is: towel on rack.

Reinforcement: pull a bead on tagulator hung on the towel rack.

*In this scenario, the learner may be alone in the bathroom when the tag point is performed. Although no one is physically there to tag as the towel is placed on the rack, the learner can say "tag" and pull a bead.

▼ TAG—Focus Funnel—tagulator on backpack

The objective is: put your homework in your backpack as soon as it is finished so you don't forget to bring it to school.

The instructions are: put your homework in the backpack, zip it up, and show a parent.

The tag point is: show parent.

Reinforcement: pull a bead on the tagulator hooked onto your backpack.

5.2.1 TAGteach Tale: Reinforce: Teenage Swearing Habit

Theresa McKeon
TAGteach International, LLC

At seventeen, my son developed the habit of swearing. At first, it was just a little four-letter word here and there, and I would just roll my eyes or say, "Matt!" as a sign of displeasure. Before long, as many habits do, the swearing became more prolific. One evening, our family was in a restaurant and Matt let the "S-bomb" fly. The table next to us had small children who heard the curse word and said, "Mommy, that's a bad word, right?" I wanted to hide under the table. Even Matthew was embarrassed. He admitted he didn't even realize he'd said the word. We both decided it was time to nix the swearing (at least in public).

Together, we came up with a "tag game." I've found many learners are happy to use TAGteach when it's presented as a game. The rules were a bit unorthodox, but—spoiler alert—Matt had his swearing under control in a single day.

The point of the game was to make him aware of his language, and then decide if it was appropriate for the setting. So, while at home, if a swear word started to come out, Matt had to stop before he finished the word and quickly change it to a different word. When he collected 10 "tags," I would give him money for one gallon of gas. (By the way, there is hardly a greater motivator than gas money for a teenager that drives.)

It sounded something like this:

Matt: "Aww sh*—" he'd screech to a halt mid-word. "I mean sugar! I just dropped my sandwich."

I would yell: "Tag!" from wherever I was in the house, and we'd end up laughing hysterically.

He ended up with two free gallons of gas by the end of the day (collecting twenty tags), but, *all swearing aside*, we both agreed that what was most reinforcing was "the game." Plus, we were both proud that we could work on an issue together. That's what was most reinforcing to me as a parent.

▼ TAG—Focus Funnel

The objective is: be aware enough to control the content of your language (in public settings in our case).

The instructions are: when you start to say a swear word—switch it to a different word.

The tag point is: switch.

Reinforcement: 10 tags = money for 1 gallon of gas.

5.3 Tag Tokens

Individual tags can be made tangible with tokens or used as currency in a "tag store." As mentioned, I set up a tag store for my gymnasts. The store was stocked with items that were donated by parents, the gym owner, and myself. Some were simply rare privileges that now could be purchased with the result of hard work (tags). Some athletes were keen to use their tags at the end of the day and some saved them for weeks in order to buy a very "expensive" item. Here are some examples of store items and their "price tags":

Stickers = 10 tags

Workout with their choice of music in the background = 50 tags

Time-off cards = 100 tags (time off from scheduled practice)

Free practice = 100 tags (practice without comments from coach)

Athletic tape = 200 tags

Workout with a friend = 200 tags

New leotard = 1,000 tags

5.4 Tiered Reinforcement

More complex reinforcement plans can be used to help sustain interest over a longer time span and allow the use of more substantial ultimate rewards.

5.4.1 TAGteach Tale: Tiered Reinforcement—the Pizza Party

Beth Wheeler
TAGteach Cofounder
Owner, A Dancer's Dream studio
Marblehead, Massachusetts

We used the Pizza Party as a long-term plan for reinforcement with the dancers at our studio. Teachers cut out pizza ingredients for each student from colored paper.

Each dancer was able to trade in tags for pieces to their own pretend pizza. As they earned each ingredient, they taped them to an area of the wall we designated The Pizza Store.

20 tags = pizza crust

10 tags = tomato sauce

10 tags = 1 pepperoni

When each dancer's pretend pizza was complete, the whole class got to enjoy a real pizza party. If someone was lagging behind with his or her pizza ingredient collection, the others helped that student earn more tags.

5.5 Reinforcement—a Rich, Complex Science

The science of reinforcement coincides with the science of learning, which is the foundation of TAGteach. Below are some of our favorite books on the subject.

- *Bringing Out the Best in People: How to Apply the Astonishing Power of Positive Reinforcement* by Aubrey Daniels.

- *The Science of Consequences: How They Affect Genes, Change the Brain, and Impact Our World* by Susan M. Schneider and René C. Reyes.

6 TAGteach in Action

We've covered the basics of the TAGteach triangle, discussed each side separately, and looked at examples. Let's see how all of the TAGteach tools come together.

6.1 Sports

6.1.1 Nag vs. TAG—Communication on the Volleyball Court

-Nag

Coach: "Girls! I can't believe you just let that ball land. I know you all thought someone else was going to get it, but this is why I keep telling you to call out "Got it!" when you are going for the ball. That will keep it from dropping or all of you from crashing into one another. Please, please, please, call "Got it.""

▼ TAG—Focus Funnel

The objective is: communicate on the court.

The instructions are: when you decide to go for the ball, call "Got it!"

The tag point is: "Got it!"

6.1.2 Nag vs. TAG—Serving the Volleyball

-Nag

Coach: "You've got to step into the ball to get more power. No! Don't step with your back foot. Step with your front foot. That is why we have all of our weight on the back foot so that you can step forward with the front foot towards the ball. Remember, you want to come into the ball with that front foot just after you toss it. It's almost at the same time. Well, the toss is just a half second before the step.

TAG—Focus Funnel

The objective is: gain power in the serve by stepping forward towards the ball.

The instructions are: after you toss the ball, step forward with the front foot.

The tag point is: step forward with front foot.

6.1.3 Nag vs. TAG—Blocking on the Football Field

-Nag

Coach: "Don't tackle someone with your head lowered. It can get you injured. Not only that, but you might get a penalty, and we'll lose yards for something I've told you not to do a million times."

TAG—Focus Funnel

The objective is: keep your head up during a tackle.

The instructions are: on the whistle, block the player in front of you.

The tag point is: contact with shoulder pad.

Reinforcement plan: Incremental success—players are typically motivated to succeed, please their coach, and to avoid injury.

6.1.4 Nag vs. TAG—Skydiving

-Nag

Instructor: "Okay, focus now. When we go to jump out of the plane, it's very important you keep your head up and back. This will help keep our center of gravity level, so we don't start to spiral or flip. If that happens, we'll have trouble getting to the parachute. Don't worry, because if you just do what I say, you'll be okay.

"Now, when I say to move forward just scoot on your bottom toward the exit of the plane. Then I'll tell you to step out onto the step that is just outside the door. When you do that, I'll put my foot out on the step and then we'll count to three, then push forward away from the plane so we don't get tangled. That's a bad thing—getting tangled. Just step out and I'll do the rest. Okay, let's suit up and get going. Just remember what I said about keeping your head back and all and you'll be fine."

▼ TAG—Focus Funnel

The objective is: proper head position, which is vital for a safe jump.

The instructions are: move toward the exit of the plane and onto the step just outside the door, and then count to three and jump away from the plane. When jumping, keep your head back.

The tag point is: head back.

Reinforcement plan: The student may be motivated by the opportunity to focus on a single goal and the sense of security that brings, particularly with something as extreme as skydiving.

6.2 Corporate Training

6.2.1 Nag vs. TAG—on a Customer Implementation Call

-Nag

Trainer: "Last time you led the implementation call, the customer dragged you down a rabbit hole in the middle of your presentation. We really need you to take control of the meeting and get the information delivered in a timelier manner. You have to get through all the important information early in the call, in case one of the key players has to leave the meeting. But remember not to be rude or make the client feel as if they don't have any input. Okay, so next time, make sure you keep everyone on track."

▼ TAG—Focus Funnel

The objective is: keep non-critical comments until the end of the call. When a client brings up non-critical issues, explain that you will write the comments down and return to them after the critical information has been covered.

The instructions are: as you are writing down the customer comments, verbalize this to the client.

The tag point is: verbalize customer comments.

Reinforcement plan: Employee is highly motivated to succeed. Achieving a well-defined goal will likely be reinforcing, especially if the manager is present or will be immediately advised of the success.

6.3 Parenting

6.3.1 Nag vs. TAG—at the Dinner Table

-Nag

Dad: "I've told you a million times to put those darn phones away. I swear I'm going to take them away for a week next time I see them at the dinner table."

▼ TAG—Focus Funnel

The objective is: to get family members to converse with each other over dinner, as opposed to being on their phones.

The instructions are: when you come to the table, drop your electronics in the basket.

The tag point is: electronics in the basket.

Reinforcement plan: A tagulator has been attached to the basket. Each family member pulls a bead after putting the electronic device in the basket. When all beads have been pulled, the family can start eating, which can be reinforcing depending on the talent of the cook. Or, when all the beads are pulled, a dollar goes into the basket. Then, when enough money is collected they can go out for ice cream.

6.3.2 Nag vs. TAG—Teenagers and the Gaming Controller

-Nag

Brother: "Mom! Brent was the last one to use the game controller and now I can't find it. You said the next person that loses the controller has to wash the car and do the dishes. Well, Brent lost it. Brent, where's the controller? Mom, make Brent find the controller and wash the car and do the dishes!"

▼ TAG—Focus Funnel

The objective is: keep the game controller on the coffee table in front of the television and game console.

*Mom found a picture of the controller, printed it, and taped it to the coffee table.

The instructions are: when finished playing, put the controller (real) on the controller (picture).

The tag point is: controller on controller.

Reinforcement plan: A tagulator is taped to the coffee table. When the real controller is placed on the picture of the controller, the player can pull a bead. When 10 beads have been pulled (well, only the teenager knows what is really reinforcing, so ask them!).

6.3.3 Nag vs. TAG—for Kids and Chores

-Nag

Mom: Stephanie, your party is going to start in a couple of hours and you need to clean your room. You don't want people to think you live in a pig sty. Go put your toys away and I'll be there in a few minutes to check on you."

Fifteen minutes later....

"Stephanie! I said to put your toys away. Why are you coloring? Your friends will be here soon! Let's go, let's go!"

Ten minutes later....

"Stephanie! I told you to put away the coloring book and clean up your toys. Now you have to hurry."

Five minutes later....

"Stephanie! If these toys aren't put away in the next five minutes, you're not having your party. Now please do what I asked."

Four minutes later....

"Stephanie! People are here! I can't believe you are still messing around! Forget it now—go downstairs and say hello to Grandma."

▼ TAG—Focus Funnel

The objective is: have a clean room before the party starts.

The instructions are: pick up toys and put it into the toy box.

The tag point is: toys in toy box.

- Stephanie picks up a toy and puts in in the toy box.
- Mom marks the moment the toy is in the toy box with a "click."
- Stephanie smiles upon hearing the click.

- Stephanie picks up two more toys and places them in the toy box.

- Mom tags at the moment each toy is in the toy box.

- Mom hands Stephanie a tagulator with a clicker on it and says, "I have to get dressed for the party. Each time you put a toy in the toy box 'click' and pull a bead. When you've pulled all ten beads, come and show me."

- As mom leaves to get dressed, she hears clicks and giggles.

- Stephanie runs into her mom's room with the tagulator. "Look, Mom, I pulled all ten beads and all of my toys are in the toy box!"

- Mom smiles and tells Stephanie that she did a great job cleaning her room for the party and that she should show Grandma the clean room when she arrives.

- Stephanie agrees with a smile.

Reinforcement plan: the opportunity to use the clicker; the opportunity to use the tagulator; Mom's love and attention; and possibly Grandma's love and attention.

Now that the toys were quickly put away and both Mom and daughter are still in a productive mood, they can practice gift-receiving etiquette before the guests arrive.

6.3.4 Nag vs. TAG—Party Manners Practice

-Nag

Mom: "Stephanie, you're five years old today and that's old enough to remember to use your manners at your birthday party. Make sure you don't forget to say thank you when your guests give you a gift, or if they say something nice. People will think you have such nice manners. Okay? You look so pretty. The guests will be here soon, so don't forget what I told you, okay? Oh, and don't forget to give Grandma a hug when she gets here. What have you got on your hands? Quick, go upstairs and wash your hands. Don't forget to use soap."

 TAG—Focus Funnel

The objective is: show good manners after receiving a birthday gift (not verbalized to Stephanie).

The instructions are: When someone hands you a gift, say thank you. When you collect five tags, you can turn them in for a sticker for your book.

The tag point is: say thank you.

- Mom hands Stephanie a pretend gift and says, "Happy Birthday!"
- Stephanie says, "Thank you!"
- Mom tags the action with a "click."
- Stephanie smiles.
- Mom repeats, handing Stephanie a "gift."
- Stephanie says, "Thank you!"
- Mom tags the action and repeats the scenario three more times.
- Stephanie states, "I got five more tags!"
- Mom says, "You have enough for a sticker for your book! And I think you're ready to be a great host at your party!"

Reinforcement plan: the opportunity to use the clicker; the opportunity to use the tagulator; Mom's love and attention; and counting tags as a token system to exchange for a sticker.

6.4 Training Surgeons

6.4.1 Nag vs. TAG—Oscillating Saw Training for Orthopaedic Surgical Residents

-Nag

Instructor: "Don't let the bone dust clog up the blade when sawing. You need to remember to keep withdrawing the blade just a bit as you're sawing so that doesn't happen. It can cause all kinds of trouble, so keep pulling it out every once in a while. Now! Withdraw! See how it clogs? You've got to remember to withdraw it more. You do not want the blade to clog when you do this on real bone. Ah, you're tilting the blade, too. You've got to keep it straight. Yep, it's clogged. I told you that would happen."

▼ TAG—Focus Funnel

The objective is: remove bone dust continuously by withdrawing the blade repeatedly while cutting a bone.

The instructions are: every two seconds, withdraw the blade one centimeter.

The tag point is: withdraw blade.

Reinforcement plan: Surgical students are typically highly motivated to succeed. Achieving a well-defined goal will likely be reinforcing enough, especially if a mentor is present or is advised of the success.

6.5 In the Classroom

6.5.1 TAG for Attention to Punctuation

-Nag

Teacher: "Ray, does what you just read sound a little strange to you? Because you didn't pay attention to the comma again, it sounded like you told us to 'Be sure to eat Grandma.' That's not the way it reads if you pause for the comma. It should sound like this. 'Be sure to eat, Grandma.' I want you to look back over the sentence and make certain that you pause where there is a comma. This is really important, as you're still reading right through them." Now sit up straight, put your feet flat on the floor, and let's try it again."

▼ TAG—Focus Funnel

The objective is: when reading out loud, pause when encountering a comma.

The instructions are: Read the sentences in this paragraph. Each time you see a comma, tap it twice with your finger, then continue reading.

The tag point is: tap comma twice.

Reinforcement plan: the student may be motivated by the opportunity to focus on a single goal and the success the sound of the tag communicates.

Tagulator to count tags—moving the bead would also increase the pause after encountering the comma.

Tiered—When all beads are pulled, exchange for a sticker, which could be accumulated and exchanged for free time, time with friends, or a chance to switch seats to be near a friend in class, etc.

6.5.2 TAG for Attention to Personal Space

-Nag

Teacher: "Sean, stop pushing! Go to the back of the line, and if you touch anyone else, you won't go outside for recess. Every day we go through this. I'm not going to tell you again."

▼ TAG—Focus Funnel

The objective is: line up for recess in an orderly fashion.

The instructions are: when you line up, stop on the next available "star target" on the floor.

The tag point is: stop on star.

- Each child lines up individually.

- The first child stops on the "star target."

- As the child stops on the target, the teacher acknowledges the action with a verbal "tag."

- Then, that student tags the next student when s/he performs the action "stop on star," and so on.

Reinforcement plan: The teacher has placed a giant tagulator on the doorframe. As each "tag" happens, the teacher pulls down a large bead (or ball). When all of the balls have been pulled, the class can go to lunch.

7 TAGteach Is for Everyone

In addition to the TAGteach triangle, there are tools you can use to increase the likelihood of success.

- TEACHER TAGS TEACHER
- LEARNER TAGS TEACHER
- PEER TAGGING
- SELF-TAGGING

7.1.1 Teacher Tags Teacher

If a picture is worth a thousand words, a demonstration is priceless. When possible, use demonstration to reduce the amount of verbal description needed and to draw the learner to the action.

During a demonstration, teachers can tag themselves as they perform a tag point, while the learner observes. This encourages the learner to observe and assess without pressure to perform.

Teachers can tag themselves using:

- a clicker if you have a free hand;
- a tongue click (a pop sound made with the tongue and the roof of the mouth);
- saying "Tag" in a neutral tone.

7.1.2 Teacher Tags Teacher—for Solving Division Problems in Math Class

Miss Sara identifies that Kyle has again forgotten to "carry over" a number while performing an addition problem. She decides to remind Kyle of the process with a demonstration and a "teacher tags teacher" game.

Miss Sara: "Let's play a tag game, Kyle. I'll go first, and you watch."

Miss Sara delivers the focus funnel to herself (and by way of demonstration, to Kyle).

▼ TAG—Focus Funnel

"**The instructions are:** when there is a carry-over number, put it in the proper column and circle it.

The tag point is: circle the carry-over number."

Miss Sara performs the addition, carries over the number and circles it. At the moment she begins to circle the number, she says, "Tag."

Miss Sara performs the next problem and carries over the number but doesn't circle it.

Kyle says, "You have to circle it!"

Miss Sara replies, "You're right."

She returns to the problem and as she begins to circle the number, she says, "Tag."

7.1.3 Learner Tags Teacher

A learner can tag the teacher! This technique puts very little pressure on the learner to perform, while still acquiring an understanding of the skill. It's also an opportunity for the teacher to assess student comprehension.

If a learner tags (or withholds the tag) at the appropriate time, the teacher can be confident the tag point was understood. If a learner tags (or withholds the tag) inappropriately, this shows that the learner is uncertain and may need additional instruction, or a different tag point.

7.1.4 Learner Tags Teacher—for More Success in Math Class

▼ TAG—Focus Funnel

The objective is: to remember to carry over the number when performing math problems.

The instructions are: when there is a carry-over number, put it in the proper column and circle it.

The tag point is: circle the carry-over number.

Miss Sara: "Okay, Kyle, your turn to tag. Give me the tag point."

Kyle: "**The tag point is:** circle the carry-over number."

Miss Sara performs the math problem, carries over the number into the proper column, and circles it.

Kyle tags as she begins the circle.

Miss Sara finishes the circle, performs the next math problem, carries over the number into the proper column, but does not circle it.

Kyle: (does not tag). "**The tag point is:** circle the carry-over number. You have to circle it!"

Miss Sara circles the carry-over number and Kyle tags. She is more confident that Kyle understands the tag point.

Kyle tags three more times as Miss Sara circles each carry-over number.

Miss Sara: Okay, it's my turn to tag. **The tag point is:** circle the carry-over number."

Miss Sara tags as Kyle performs five more math problems with 100 percent success.

Miss Sara: "Well done, Kyle. You've become a master at this. Will you play this same tag game with Ryan?"

7.2 Peer Tagging

Teachers are not the only ones who have the opportunity to tag. Because tag points are a single action, observable and objective, in many cases, a learner can tag other learners.

Students virtually double their learning experience as they look for/focus on the correct action in their partner in order to tag it. Competition and criticism often turn into cooperation and empathy when students are given the responsibility for tagging success.

Benefits

- **Mental practice:** Coaches know that mental practice is nearly as important as physical practice. When learners tag each other, they get a great mental workout.

- **Efficient training time:** When learners tag each other, everyone is tagging or receiving tags. Everyone is focused on the skill.

- **Low-stress environment:** The learner can focus on the actual mechanics of the skill without the initial pressure of having to perform in front of a person of authority.

- **Responsibility:** Many learners revel in the responsibility of teaching others.

- **Engaging injured players**: Peer tagging is the perfect opportunity for injured players to participate. Rather than just sitting and watching, an injured athlete can mentally train by watching carefully and tagging others.

- **Equal attention:** All learners receive positive feedback equally, including the "shadow" student, the quiet learners, who may fall under the coach's radar.

- **Teacher freedom:** The coach is freed to work with a learner, who may be having issues and could use a little one-on-one time, or to move from group to group giving guidance.

7.2.1 Peer Tagging—for Gymnastics

It's not surprising that gymnasts occasionally get injured. Usually, it's a minor injury that, with a few days off to rest, will mend itself. But gymnasts aren't known for their love of sitting around. How do you keep them working, but still rest the injury? Have them tag their teammate's skills!

Coach Julie: "That ankle looks much better, Laura. Only a few more days and you'll be ready to practice again. For now, can you help Kelsey with full turns on beam? Tag five times for 'toe to ankle' and five times for 'airplane arms.'"

Laura: "Sure. Come on, Kelsey, there's an open beam over here."

Coach Julie: "Oh, and Kelsey, can you think of a tag point that Laura can do sitting down?"

Kelsey: "Sure, do you want to practice hollow holds? Maybe the tag point could be: shoulders to ears?"

Laura: "Okay."

Coach Julie: "Sounds good—go to it, girls."

7.2.2 TAGteach Tale: Peer Tagging for Practicing Presentations

Charlene Nelson, Principal, Mercer Health & Benefits Administration,
LLC
Des Moines, Iowa

Our team is responsible for implementing benefit programs at large corporations. This means the team must gather and share a large amount of information with multiple groups.

We used TAGteach to slow down our conversations, giving the listener time to hear and understand the many different types of information we discussed.

During training, a focus funnel helped to organize the moment of learning and having the team peer tag, made the exercise time efficient.

▼ TAG—Focus Funnel

The objective is: when delivering important information over the phone, give your listener time to process by providing a pause.

The instructions are: Following a critical statement, hold for a count of three. Raise one finger for each silent count.

The tag point is: count.

Reinforcement plan. Employees are highly motivated to succeed. Achieving a well-defined goal will likely be reinforcing, especially if the manager is present or will be immediately advised of the success.

Note: The adults knew how to count to three, *remembering* to count was the skill. The tag point "count" was created to provide a physical manifestation of "remember."

- The action was tagged the instant the learner started counting instead of at the end of the count of three.

- Displaying a finger for each count made the action observable, even when they counted silently to themselves.

We worked in groups of two. One team member practiced the script, while the other tagged "count."

Below are two script examples where a tag point was used. Places to *count* are represented with (...).

"On today's call, there are three critical pieces of information (...). They are (...)"

A pause was placed after each critical topic was listed.

"To complete the project on time (...) we will need your final product decisions by December 2 (...) Will you be able to meet that date?"

7.3 Using All of the Above

7.3.1 All of the Above—Brushing Teeth and the Joy of Spitting

Part 1: Teacher Tags Teacher

Paul is helping his daughter Abbey perfect the art of brushing her teeth. Abbey has conquered the brush part and is ready to move onto the somewhat tricky act of spitting.

Dad invites Abbey to watch him "spit." In order to make the step obvious and a bit more fun, Dad has placed a smiley-face sticker in the sink. This will be a target for the spit. Dad gathers the stepstool, toothbrushes, a metal clicker, and, of course, Abbey. Once everything is set up, he demonstrates with the teacher tags teacher system.

▼ TAG—Focus Funnel

The objective is: spit on the target after brushing.

The instructions are: after brush, brush, brush, spit toothpaste-on-sticker.

The tag point is: spit!

Reinforcement plan: Dad thinks playing a "game" will be reinforcing. He will also leave the smiley face sticker in the sink.

- Dad holds the toothbrush in one hand and the clicker in the other.

- He brush, brush, brushes, and as he spits on the target, he tags himself: click!

- Again, he brush, brush, brushes, and tags himself as he spits: click!

- Next, he throws in a little trick to check if Abbey really understands the tag point and to see if she is paying attention.

- Dad brush, brush, brushes, doesn't spit, and doesn't click.

- Abbey laughs and says, "Spit, Daddy!"

- Dad "remembers" the tag point and spits: click!

- This is good information for Dad. Abbey understands "spit" is the tag point.

Part 2: Student Tags Teacher

- Dad hands the clicker to Abbey.

- Dad asks Abbey, "What's the tag point?"

- Abbey answers, "Spit! **The tag point is:** spit!"

- Dad brush, brush, brushes and then leans into the sink to spit.

- Abbey tags as he spits. *Dad notes the appropriate tag.

- Then Dad brush, brush, brushes and leans into the sink, but doesn't spit.

- Abbey looks and says, "No tag." *Dad notes the appropriate no-tag.

- Dad then spits.

- Abbey tags.

- They repeat the exercise a few times.

The Joy of Spitting, Part 3: Teacher Tags Student

Dad hands Abbey her toothbrush and takes the clicker. "Okay, Abbey," he says. "Your turn."

Abbey states the instructions and tag point: "After, I brush, brush, brush, I spit toothpaste-on-sticker. **The tag point is**: spit!"

- Abbey brush, brush, brushes, and then spits.
- Dad tags.
- **"The tag point is:** spit!" Abbey says. She likes this game and does it four more times.

The Joy of Spitting, Part 4: Peer Tagging

- Abbey says, "I can tag Charlie for spit!"
- Dad smiles and says, "That's nice, Abbey, but Charlie is only two months old!"

"Peer tagging lets you be the teacher, and you feel good about helping your teammates do better."

—Chelsea, a ten-year-old cheerleader at Sun Valley Elementary

7.4 Self-Tagging

We all have skills to change or perfect, and quite often no one is around to "coach" us. And quite frankly there are times when we just don't want to be coached.

With self-tagging, we use the same clear, efficient, positive tools to prepare our own learning environment. After all, we should be teaching ourselves with the same respect with which we teach others.

- **Identify the goal and create a tag point**: make sure it follows the WOOF model.

- **Tag success**: This can actually include sound from a marker or maybe a fist pump, thumbs up, big 'ole grin, a shout of glee, or just a thought: *I did it!* Tagulators are perfect for documenting your success in a manner observable by you and others.

- **Reinforce**: As always, what is reinforcing is determined by the individual. For many of us, the act of providing evidence (tagulator) of our undertaking creates motivation to do that desirable act again.

7.4.1 Self-Tagging—to Remember Your Cell Phone

...For when you just can't remember to unplug your cell phone from the car charger when you exit the car.

▼ TAG—Focus Funnel

The objective is: remember to take your phone when you leave the car.

The instructions are: put car in park and then reach for the phone.

The tag point is: grab phone.

Reinforcement: Pull a bead on the tagulator hanging on the gear shift or in the side pocket on the door. After 10 beads are pulled—buy yourself a fancy coffee.

7.4.2 Self-Tagging—for Healthy Snacking

...For choosing raw fruits and vegetables or nuts from the refrigerator, instead of processed snacks.

▼ TAG—Focus Funnel

The objective is: to be mindful when eating, which will eventually lead to healthy eating.

The instructions are: open refrigerator door and choose a healthy snack.

The tag point is: make a choice.

Reinforcement plan: A five-bead tagulator on the fridge door works great. When all five beads are pulled, create a new tag point, perhaps: choose anything raw.

Note: I made this an easy first tag point. The "choice" might start out as a meatball over a celery stick, but it is an achievable first step toward mindful eating.

7.4.3 TAGteach Tale: Self-Tagging and Parenting

Keri Gorman, Educator, Mom
Portland, Oregon

I frequently use tag points to help my young son, Max, learn how to do something, like rock climb, tap dance, or ride his bike. If I'm really sharp, I can even use a tag points during moments of frustration, like bedtime, dinnertime, or having to leave the playground. Occasionally, Max tests my ability to think in a behaviorally rational way or to think rationally at all if I'm being totally honest. This is when I give myself a tag point. I remember a certain lunchtime experience...

I just wanted the toys picked up and for Max to sit down at the table. There was resistance. It was not a good day for that. My to-do list was a mile long—I had to get ready for work, the dog was barking, and my inner child was about to start yelling.

 TAG—Focus Funnel

The objective is: stop and assess the situation with my child instead of just reacting.

The instructions are: when Max isn't listening to me or is challenging my instructions, take a breath and regroup.

The tag point is: assess.

Reinforcement plan: Pull a bead on my tagulator. Show the tagulator to my husband before bed to let him know how many times I tried to be calm.

The tag point (for me) was: assess.

I said, "Tag!" to myself and pulled a bead as I sifted through the options.

Choices:

- I could raise my voice.
- I could remove the toys.
- I could let him know to come to the table or he would miss eating lunch.
- I could go to another room and scream into a pillow.
- I could bring lunch to the playroom and have a "picnic."
- I could think up a "tag on the fly" to get Max to listen.

Not gonna lie, after assessing, I chose to say, "Lunch is on the table and I will remove it if you choose to stay in your room!" Luckily, according to the TAGteach methodology, I still win. I assessed the situation (didn't explode) and then decided to take the easy way out. Hey, it happens.

7.4.4 TAGteach Tale: Self Tagging—Waiting Tables with ADHD

Matt McKeon, Server

90

Charlotte, North Carolina

I'm twenty-two years old and I'm a server at an upscale sushi bar and restaurant, and also a full-time college student. I have many tasks to remember throughout the day. Today, for example, I have to press my work clothes, research for a term paper, post on the discussion board for my online classes, send in my car insurance payment, and then, when I get to work, I'll have to remember drink orders, and appetizer orders, and special notes from people with food allergies, etc.

I've also been diagnosed with ADHD. I constantly have to readjust my focus and attention to not get lost in the myriad of thoughts. I understand that this is something many people struggle with on a daily basis—and there are ways to train yourself on your day-to-day tasks.

The first step is to identify your problem.

For example, I was having an issue remembering to enter the customer's order after taking it. This was causing me some serious stress because I would regularly have to ask the chef to rush an order because I'd spaced out and forgot to put the order into the computer.

The solution to this problem was simple: I had to enter in the order immediately after receiving it from the guest—not grab drinks for another table I saw waiting at the bar, not fill water glasses. I had to go to computer no matter what. But in addition to tasks, sometimes people ask for directions to the bathroom, or a table asks me to find their waitress, or the chef is yelling out that three orders are ready to be taken out. Other people run into similar problems every day and find themselves confronted with the same instruction: "Just do it."

"Just do it?" Obviously, if all I needed was someone to tell me to "just do it," I wouldn't have been having the problem in the first place. I needed restructuring. I needed a clear and simple goal. I needed to make that goal a priority, and I needed to execute the goal.

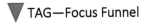 TAG—Focus Funnel

The objective is: stay focused through distraction until the order is punched into the computer.

The instructions are: say thank you to the customer, then punch the order into the computer.

The tag point is: punch it in.

(I snapped my fingers as an audible tag.)

Reinforcement plan: Pull a bead on the tagulator hanging from my waiter's apron. That small show of my success was very reinforcing.

I used the tag point to unclutter my thoughts. Every time I entered in an order, immediately after saying, "Thank you," I snapped my fingers (as an audible tag) and pulled a bead on the tagulator hanging from my waiter's apron.

Since I started using TAGteach at my workplace, there have been some significant positive changes in my efficacy.

TAGteach is not just for one person to use to teach another; it's also an approach to learning and retraining for ourselves.

7.4.5 TAGteach Tale: Self-Tagging—for Fear of Flying

Eva Bertilsson, Cofounder, Carpe Momentum
Coauthor of *Agility Right from the Start*
Uddevalla, Sweden

I'm not at all thrilled about flying. I pretty much avoid looking out the windows, especially on the way up. I just hate knowing how far from the ground I am and the feeling of going higher and higher. So, I try to focus on other things or pretend I'm on the ground.

On one of the many flights I have to take for work, I did my best not to look out the window during the takeoff. After a couple of minutes, I gave looking out of the window a try—not pleasant. I looked away and tried again a few minutes later—again, not pleasant. This is what

I went through every time I was on a plane. Then a thought crossed my mind; "Train it!" So, I created a tag point.

The tag point is: glance out window.

I glanced out and gave myself a mental click, followed by looking away from the window. I counted the tags to keep myself busy. After six, I decided to vary the duration.

The tag point is: one-second glance.

Tag—look away.

The tag point is: three-second glance.

Tag—look away, and so on.

I realized that before, I had been looking away as soon as I felt uncomfortable, which was very reinforcing. This time I concentrated on adding seconds and then tagging, which made me keep looking for a second longer, even when it felt uncomfortable—which actually made it possible for the discomfort to come and go while I was still looking out the window. Yippee!

Within half an hour (100 tags), I had a duration of up to thirty seconds of actually looking out—looking at the ground, the clouds, the wing of the plane, etc. In addition, every turn or bump worked as a cue to look out of the window, instead of the other way around.

Then I switched to reinforcing myself with music—music on while looking out, music off while doing other things (talking, eating, etc.). This worked fine, and it kept me looking out most of the time. I felt practically no discomfort.

We landed, and I transferred to another plane. Now I had to test my new skill at a greater challenge: takeoff and going up, up, up. I lowered the criteria and tagged for one-to-five seconds of looking. This worked great, and I had zero latency pretty much all the time. (I never actually looked away; I merely closed my eyes for a split second.)

I didn't feel uncomfortable for more than maybe half a second at a time! So, I quit tagging and just enjoyed looking out the window for the rest of the flight. I counted to three and tagged myself the few times it felt slightly unpleasant (like when there were bumps or strange noises from the plane).

I was so proud of myself when we reached the destination! Now, I actually look forward to flying again. Self-tagging created courage and squashed my fear of flying.

Bonus: it was neat to see the landscape and the clouds from above!

8 Flying without the Funnel

There are times when you may choose not to use the formal focus funnel language or are unable to use words at all. Fortunately, we have tools for that. In this chapter, we will learn about:

- CAPTURING

- SHORT-PHRASE INSTRUCTIONS

- NONE OF THE ABOVE

8.1 Capturing

There are times when verbal communication, no matter how well constructed, is of little value. For example, if:

- you and your student speak different languages;

- your student has limited or no ability to use verbal language;

- your student is too young to speak or understand verbal language;

- demonstration is not an option;

- an exact physical position or movement that is too difficult to define verbally.

In these circumstances, you may choose to forgo using the verbal focus funnel and use the "capture" method instead.

Capturing is pretty much just how it sounds. The teacher waits for the student to perform the action naturally or by setting up the environment to promote the action. When the student executes the action, it is tagged and reinforced, encouraging the action to happen again.

The process of capturing an action may have to be repeated numerous times until the student connects the action with the tag and the reinforcer. Once this happens, the behavior should start happening more often. At this point, it may possible to assign the action a name.

8.1.1 TAGteach Tale: Capturing Eye Contact

Seany Pogson, Parent of a child with Autism
Greater Manchester, England

Teachers remarked how well Tink (my daughter with autism) was engaging with people and the improved eye contact she was using. We have done nothing complicated, just captured any attempt at eye contact with a tag and then immediately delivered reinforcement.

Gradually, we shaped (built step by step) this behavior, so that it became more and more frequent. Now Tink is starting to make eye contact more and more in natural environments. Using the tag to mark the behavior, which delivers immediate feedback, and then using positive reinforcement has been the key.

"What magic is this, which captures the rare moment of a fleeting glance from a child who won't give eye contact? Then by its own laws makes that moment happen again to the wonder of those who saw it, too."

8.1.2 TAGteach Tale: Capturing—for Movement and Direction

Martha Gabler, Author of *Chaos to Calm: Using TAGteach to*
Overcome the Challenges of Autism
Washington, DC

My son is now a teenager. When he was three years old, he was diagnosed with severe autism. He was profoundly nonverbal. We struggled and suffered for many years, becoming increasingly isolated from normal, everyday life. I was desperate to improve his skills so that we could go out in the community, go to the grocery store, or take a walk in the park.

Life changed for the better after I learned about capturing with the TAGteach method. The acoustic support or "tag" allowed for communication without verbal language. With one quick click, I could say, "Hey, that was great!" I frequently added a treat right after the click to reinforce the behavior and the tagging process. The tag got around my son's many problems of sensory overload, auditory processing, and aversion to language.

My first target behavior was "two steps in same direction." (My son was so chaotic when we were outside that I first had to teach him to walk in a straight line.) I observed my son's walking behavior, and when he took two steps in the same direction, I tagged and give him a treat. He learned very quickly, and he had the freedom to learn at his own pace.

I could not "force" the behavior, but whenever he took two steps in the same direction, I identified, highlighted, and reinforced. He experienced neither coercion nor punishment. He didn't suffer from being overwhelmed by too much demand. If my son couldn't perform a behavior, it was my job to think about it and break down the task into a smaller, more accessible part. Within a period of five months, my son went from not being able to walk in a straight line for even two steps, to going on five-mile hikes in wilderness settings.

8.1.3 TAGteach Tale: Capturing—"Use Your Core"

Beth Wheeler
TAGteach Cofounder
Owner, A Dancer's Dream studio
Marblehead, MA

You hear it in dance classes, at the gym, heck a nurse said it to me when I was delivering my son: "Use your core!" There are lots of muscles that make up the "core" and so, especially for a beginner, engaging them really doesn't mean anything. A student tried to define it once for me as, "Some absent feeling somewhere in the stomach maybe?" And yet coaches still shout, "Work that core!" They shout it over and over. Once we initiated TAGteach at the studio, it was such a relief to be able to simply capture the moment our students engaged their core. They didn't even realize they were doing it. But, the "click" sound offered an instantaneous, "Yes, what you are doing right now is perfect." I also love that the clicker doesn't require the learner to verbally communicate. They get to stay in a "learning bubble." Instead of commenting, they get to ask internal questions: What was I doing when I heard the click? Can I repeat that? Yes, yes, I can! And they do.

8.2 Short-Phrase Coaching

Now that you're an expert at reducing language and creating clear goals, you may want to add another tool to your kit: short-phrase coaching.

Short-phrase coaching allows the teacher to combine several previously acquired WOOF goals together in a single instruction. Because there are multiple goals, there will be no tag.

Stop! Drop! Roll! This is an example of short-phrase instructions most of us learned as kids.

The instructions are: if your clothes are on fire: stop, drop, and roll.

Short-phrase coaching helps maintain the brevity and clarity of tag points but allows us to move forward and create chains of actions that make up final skills.

8.2.1 Short-Phrase Coaching—for Petting a Dog

Experts tell us running up to a dog, even one we know, can be frightening for the dog. Here is a way to teach people to ask the dog, "Do you want me to pet you?"

*This teacher has decided to break the chain into tag points first. Once learned, she will switch to short-phrase coaching and practice the entire chain.

The instructions are: pat your thighs to invite the dog to come to you.

The tag point is: pat.

The instructions are: pat your thighs and when the dog comes over, pet him on the back.

The tag point is: pet.

The instructions are: pat your thighs and when the dog comes over, pet him on the back, and then pause to see if the dog wants you to continue.

The tag point is: pause.

You have all three steps! Let's put them together and practice with this adorable stuffed dog first.

The instructions are: if you want to pet a dog: pat-pet-pause.[9]

8.2.2   Short-Phrase Instructions—for Industrial Safety, Ear Protection

---

[9] These steps are from the video https://goo.gl/yhE1BA and http://stopthe77.com/

Believe it or not, using ear protection (earplugs) is a common "nag" point. It's easy to assume that by just telling employees to "put in your ear protection," it would be instruction enough. But proper insertion is a real skill. If earplugs are inserted improperly, they can cause discomfort and reduce earplug effectiveness.

We took the time to break down the skill and create short-phrase instructions that could be easily taught and practiced, even during safety training with large groups. The instructions were so short, we didn't need to tag any of the steps.

- Hook the ear (opens canal)
- Roll to skinny (attenuates the earplug)
- Insert into ear (gently into ear canal)
- Release ear (secures the earplug)
- Hold for ten seconds (allows earplug to properly expand)

Students quickly shortened these instructions into single word instructions. It sounded like a chant as they said and performed each step.

- Hook
- Roll
- Insert
- Release
- Hold

8.2.3 TAGteach Tale: for Orthopedic Skills Training

Martin Levy, MD
Program Director and Clinical Professor of Orthopaedic Surgery

Albert Einstein College of Medicine, Montefiore Medical Center
Bronx, New York

I've never counted but I'm sure I've used hundreds—even thousands—of words while teaching skills. Now that we use TAGteach to teach a list of core skills to fluency first, we can just chain any number of them together and quickly build a wide range of skills with minimal words and distractions.

Because each of the following component actions were in the skillset, we taught "cast-cutting" with short-phrase instructions and didn't need to individually tag any of the components.

- Brace (the saw)
- Roll (the saw)
- Contact (plaster with saw blade)
- Plunge (through plaster)
- Back (the saw) out

Short-phrase instructions and tag points work well together and can be combined to help students remember a list of instructions, and they can be used to highlight one point in particular.

For example, when teaching students to use an oscillating saw, we gave the cues and made the most important one a tag point.

The instructions are:
- Start saw before touching
- Stabilize
- Rock
- Engage
- Back out

The tag point is: start saw before touching.

The residents used peer tagging to make the best use of time and encourage cooperation.

8.3 Getting Started

8.3.1 TAGteach Tale: Tag and Talk while Practicing Archery

Luca Canever, Teacher
Verona, Italy

I've always loved archery. I just don't find the time to practice very often. One day, I found myself in an archery training center and purchased three introductory training lessons.

Day 1: I arrive at the center with all my gear and clickers in my backpack

(You never know if a tag session might break out).

The Instructor said, "Well, show me a shot."

So, I shot.

The Instructor said, "No, don't lower your head and open your mouth and don't—"

"Okay, I'll try again."

"Yes, that was better, but you do not have to do—"

"Listen, can I ask you to use something during lessons? I'll show you how it works and then we'll give it a try. Okay?"

He agreed.

Then I asked, "What is the first thing you think I need to improve?"

"You must not open your mouth."

Me: "Okay, click if my mouth is closed at the anchor point."

(The anchor point is the position that the archer reaches immediately prior to release.)

I kept my mouth shut. He clicked.

After working through a few tag points, we took some time to discuss why certain positions and postures were important. I enjoyed hearing more background information in between the tag sessions.

Day 2: As soon as I arrived at the center, I give the instructor a brand-new clicker with a tagulator. We identified three tag points and worked through them in progressions. In between the tag sessions, we had several wonderful discussions on archery and how our muscles worked while shooting.

Day 3: I arrived to find the instructor with the marker already beautifully hanging from his belt. We got right to work. By the end of the day, we found it much easier to identify and insert tag points at just the right place.

I appreciated that we were talking less about "don't do this" or "don't do that" and talking more about how the muscles must work and the importance of posture and general information about the movement and the sport.

When the three sessions were finished, I was happy and felt great about my progress.

"For someone who previously trained alone, you've made great progress," the instructor commented.

I received the compliment with joy, as my instructor set off to his next lesson.

As I headed toward the facility exit, I heard the clicker.

I think using TAGteach hit the bullseye for my instructor

9 TAGteach Success Stories

Please enjoy the following inspirational stories of teachers and students who *Tag! Don't Nag*.

9.1.1 TAGteach Tale: Music and the Magic of Tagging

Kelly Drifmeyer, Associate Professor of Horn
Crane School of Music SUNY-Potsdam

My early learning experiences as a hornist were with artist/musicians I think of as old-school teachers. They learned how to teach from their teachers, and they from theirs, back to the European Masters of the instrument. There was one right way—their way—and to not follow instructions to the letter, or to not provide the ideal result, was an invitation to a browbeating, caused embarrassment, or was demeaning (sometimes resulting in harsh verbal correction). Comments like, "You'll never be successful sounding like that," "That's not good enough," and "You'd better find a different career," were all commonplace in both my own experience and the experiences of my fellow students.

My early training (and my perfectionism) had left me with streams of self-abusive, mental chatter that turned on every time I picked up the horn. I couldn't practice, rehearse, or perform without negative thoughts flowing through my head. I almost quit the profession twice. I struggled with auditions—the one and only way to get a job in the performance field. I played beautifully at times and had meltdowns at others. Nothing was ever "good enough," so the angry commentary never stopped. Worst of all, I saw the same attitudes and negativity in my own students.

TAGteach isn't where I started, but it is where I ended up. I tried The Artist's Way, the Inner Game Books, Peak Performance ideas, even "positive speaking" models, and nothing solved the problem completely—until I picked up the clicker and started tagging. I didn't have the easiest time, but with practice came an understanding of how the language of TAGteach helped me define my own thoughts and helped my students with their own frame of reference.

I now use the approach for specific tasks with all my students. They universally respond in a positive manner, and many of them will ask for a tag session when they find they're struggling with a particular activity. It's an invaluable tool when working on high-stress or high-frustration problems. I find it to be especially effective when working on more physical issues.

Musicians frequently work with muscles on a micro level—tiny, flexible motions of tiny, fragile muscle groups. Stress and tension can ruin the ability to use these muscles correctly, and I've found tagging lowers frustration, which lowers tension, which creates a calmer, more relaxed learner and calmer muscles. And like magic, the relaxed learner is a successful doer.

The "magic" of TAGteach was really brought home because of one student in particular; Amy was bright, hardworking, and dedicated, but a mental and physical mess: She had tight, twisted posture, loads of tension, and a low threshold for frustration. She got upset at the smallest things, and I would walk on eggshells trying to get her to correct a problem without having a full-on meltdown.

I'll be honest. Amy was not my favorite student. I was irritated by her touchiness, and I'd lost patience with her meekness and sensitivity. It was no surprise that in one lesson, I found myself correcting a singular problem again and again. I was getting frustrated, my voice was getting louder, and I noticed her hunching lower and lower in her chair, getting smaller and tighter at every attempt.

"Stop," I said to both of us. I took a deep breath and picked up the clicker. "This is a clicker. When you hear this sound—(I clicked it)—you'll know you've done it right. If you don't hear the sound, just try it again, no problem." That's all I told her the first time. I took her through a focus funnel—explained what we were doing, then defined a single task, then gave her a single tag point—and off we went.

I felt silly for not having done it weeks earlier. Amy was finding success within ten minutes. And, more importantly, she was then able to successfully integrate the new skill into a larger, more complex format. She also remembered, and repeated, the newly won skill for me the next week—and the next.

What's most interesting to me about this story? I like Amy more now than I used to. We've found a way to communicate that took the friction out of our relationship. She learns more confidently, and I'm also more relaxed, knowing I can say what I need to without hurting her emotional foundation.

This is an elegant, simple, precise language I use to interact with myself and with others. It's a gateway to learning and teaching.

9.1.2 TAGteach Tale: Bridging the Language Barrier in Commercial Fishing

Tim Meintz, Business Owner
Cascade Fishing, Inc.

For our TAGteach training, we brought in mockups of the fish processing equipment, including a head-cutting machine. Back on the boat, the head-cutter did just that. It cut the heads off freshly caught fish so that they could be gutted, packed, and frozen onboard. "Bad cuts" on the fish are costly, so there's also a guy who sets the fish up so that the "header" can make the cuts quickly and safely. Lining the fish up for the most efficient cut is quite technical. The person performing the task is working at a very high speed and has to account for angle, direction, and speed of the fish going to the header. The tag points for each step were clear.

The tag point is: belly in.

The tag point is: head down.

Using these tag points to build confidence during training was great. Yelling won't make someone confident—and, in our case, it won't even make them understand since many of the crew speak English as a second language, and some don't understand it at all.

9.1.3 TAGteach Tale: I Tagged and Voilà!

Sara Geary, Dance Teacher at a Private Charter School
Boston, Massachusetts

After many happy years as a teacher at A Dancer's Dream, my dance studio in Marblehead, Massachusetts—a wonderful studio where every teacher is TAGteach certified and the children are very tag savvy—I recently branched out into the world of public education and accepted a position as a full-time dance teacher in a charter school network in Boston.

The charter school network is a high-performing, K-8 charter school with three campuses. The schools are academically rigorous, have a strict behavior policy, and are huge on positive reinforcement and behavior narration. They also have every student take dance. The dance classes are large, with 27–32 students per class. Needless to say, I have my hands full.

After a year and a half of struggling with huge classes, no mirrors, and less-than-perfect dance "studio" conditions, I asked my principal if I could start using TAGteach. She said yes, and I breathed a huge sigh of relief. I could finally introduce TAGteach and the audible marker to all my classes. Below are a few highlights from our first week using TAGteach.

First grade: There are 32 children in this class (32 children!). In an effort to streamline my classes, I decided to initially use TAGteach to work on class management. As the class began, I kept an eye out for the first scholar who quietly sat down in a crisscross.

Without saying a word, I tagged the action and voila! The room went from chaos to silence in three tags. It was so easy! They figured out right away that if they didn't get a tag, they could look at a friend who did get tagged and fix their behavior to match. My entire class was silent, ready to go—without redirection from me—in less than a minute.

One scholar told me, "I like the clicker because when you tag one person, we all know what to do without you talking and wasting our learning time." Right on, kid—me too.

Sixth grade: We are well into our tap unit. With 27 kids in this class, it's challenging to see and correct the mistakes of every child. How do you solve problems like too many kids and not enough time? With TAGteach, of course! After watching the entire class attempt flaps (a tap skill) and making a mental note of the most common errors, I chose one student to start the process. I explained what a tag is and how it helps your body and brain learn.

In less than two minutes and with only two tag points, his flaps were fixed. Not only did it fix his flaps, but everyone in the class vastly improved after watching the TAGteach session. They were thrilled and just a little amazed. The experience was a powerful reminder of the effectiveness of TAGteach.

9.1.4 TAGteach Tale: How about You Try It My Way?

Victoria Fogel, MA, BCBA, Researcher
Grand Valley State University

One day, during my five-year-old son Jack's guitar lesson, I heard him say to his teacher, "Let me show you something. This is a marshmallow counter, and this is a clicker. When I do something right on the guitar, you click this button and then I get a marshmallow. How about you try it my way?"

I always leave tag materials in his guitar case for when we practice together but never thought he would pull them out during his lesson. As the lesson was challenging and Jack was trying hard to stay focused, his teacher agreed to try the technique. When Jack finished his lesson, he came over to meet me and said, "I earned marshmallows!" He was very proud of the skills he performed to earn the marshmallows. The marshmallow reinforcer was well on its way to being replaced with the intrinsic reinforcement of knowing how to strum the strings.

Man, this stuff is good—both the TAGteach and the marshmallows.

9.1.5 TAGteach Tale: Tag points for CrossFit

Linda Randall, DVM
Cloverleaf Animal Hospital
Lodi, Ohio

I was struggling with the width of my foot placement when doing certain lifts in my CrossFit workout. I thought I was moving them to the right place, but the coach still had to correct the position. Somehow, I just didn't have the right "picture" in my head of where my feet should finish. Finally, it dawned on me to create a tag point. I had been using TAGteach for years to train my veterinary technicians to perform skills like how to place an endotracheal tube in a snake and how to gently restrain a bird for an exam. Creating a tag point for foot placement should be easy.

I placed blue painters' tape on the floor where my feet should land, and blue tape on the outside of my sneakers.

The tag point is: tape to tape.

I gave it a try. I had my training partner tag the moment my feet hit the mark. I hit the mark the very first time. After a few successes, I had the feeling for it memorized and didn't need the feedback any longer. It worked perfectly.

I've found TAGteach to be a simple and extremely effective way to improve my lifting form in small, important increments. My improved form allowed me to increase my deadlift by twenty pounds in one day.

9.1.6 TAGteach Tale: Where You Need It Most

Inmates from the Fluvanna Correctional Center for
Women on TAGteach Training
Troy, Virginia

Virginia Dare invited me to visit the Fluvanna Correctional Center for Women in Virginia so I could introduce TAGteach to specially selected inmates. Miss Dare was leading the Pen Pals program in both facilities (a program in which inmates are paired with and responsible for the training of shelter dogs). The senior inmates in the program often taught newer members the specific training techniques used in the program. The Fluvanna center and I thought that the TAGteach methodology could provide communication skills necessary in an environment when neither punishment nor lavish praise is acceptable.

The inmates were very cooperative and enthusiastic about TAGteach. The women were kind enough to take the time to provide written comments after learning about TAGteach:

"In this type of setting, it's difficult to receive feedback without looking for judgment and/or negativity. The neutrality of the TAGteach technique makes it possible. It's not so much a compliment—which can be hard for us to accept—but more of an affirmation that we are being mindful of our actions.

On the day after learning about TAGteach, I was at work teaching math and computer-aided drafting. I found myself wondering how I could TAGteach this. Instead of fussing, I started discussing. The immediate result was improved performance and mood. At the end of a fraction session, I had several women tell me this was the first time they hadn't hated math or felt stupid when dealing with it."

—Theresa

"It also made me realize that I need to start looking at the positive in my teammates. I have to rearrange my way of thinking and even communicating."

—Tracey

"Positively reinforced teachers seeing success in their students due to TAGteach become more dedicated teachers. Students being positively reinforced by pointing out (tagging) their successes will be more dedicated students. It's a wonderful positive circle!

Having taught more than half my life, I've always believed any learning should be fun. TAGteach is fun."

—Janice

"It has really helped me to focus on my issues, and instead of feeling bad when I do wrong, I now feel positive about myself when I do something right."

—Denise

9.1.7 TAGteach Tale: Medical Students Find a New Perspective with Tagging

Karen McClean, MD

The key new perspective for me is seeing how TAGteach can be applied in cognitive domains, as well as physical domains. This was a major incentive for me to learn more about TAGteach. Applications in the physical domains are easy to see. Understanding how I can use it to help students who are struggling with cognitive processing problems is more challenging, but I was able to use TAGteach very effectively to help a senior medical resident work through issues around how he presents cases—which reflects how he thinks about cases.

I have experimented with a variety of markers, from a clicker to a bell. I finally developed a Blackberry app to use in the hospital where an unobtrusive, yet distinct tag tone is needed.

I have applied the marker/reinforcement in learners from preschool age to preteen and teens, to adult learners. In particular, medical students and residents are highly reinforced by knowing they got something right and by being able to practice skills in front of peers without having to fear a verbal correction.

For all activities, "the tag point is" phraseology is used. For some activities, the entire focus funnel phrasing has been helpful and appropriate.

Existing programs in which I have integrated TAGteach:

Medical school—undergraduate training in clinical and procedural skills.

Medical residents—used to enhance training in physical exam skills.

Remedial training for internal medicine residents: developing and testing clinical reasoning and case presentations.

Key takeaway points:

- Multiple, sequential tag points are workable.

- Peer engagement through calling out the next tag point for a student engaged in the procedure offered students many opportunities to "recall" the next tag point, state it out loud, and embed it in memory.

- When doing a long, complex procedure, handing out a tag point summary at the end is appreciated.

- TAGteach is as efficient as conventional teaching in terms of time required.

- Students are quick to accept the approach when they understand how it can improve their learning.

As evidence of the success of this technique, one of my medical students sent me the following letter:

"I had never done an LP [lumbar puncture], but I went through the simulation teaching using models with my instructor during JURSI (Junior Undergrad Rotating Student Internship) orientation week. In her group, the teaching method incorporated tag points that allowed us to remember the sequence of steps in performing an LP. I had not thought about those tag points since that day we had training, which was about six months ago."

"Recently on my neurology rotation, a resident offered to let me do an LP, but first I had to explain the process, the contraindications, and indications for doing an LP. I was amazed at how easily I recalled the tag points in their correct order. The resident was impressed and let me perform the LP, which ended up being successful on the first try. I think there are many medical students that would benefit from the teaching method employed by my instructor where a procedure or physiological process is broken down into steps—tag points—that make a complicated pathway/procedure more manageable and easier to mentally process."

9.1.8 TAGteach Tale: TAGteach for the Visually Impaired

Tony Harvey,
Senior Guide Dog Mobility Practitioner,
Cardiff, Wales

I have worked with guide dogs and people who are visually impaired for the past ten years. Our job is to train people on how to work with their dog so they can have the best mobility possible. I have been using TAGteach to break down these processes and turn them into easy-to-learn chunks.

For me, it's like telling a story or painting a picture. Teach a single tag point and then add one more part and then another until you have the whole picture.

One client I recently worked with has memory issues and finds it difficult to process information. When she qualified with her dog, she said to me (unprompted), "TAGteach was great for me as I didn't have to process a lot of words. I just knew if I hadn't heard the click, I had something else to do. Thank you for understanding me."

9.1.9. TAGteach Tale: Taking Medicine Calmly

My son has to take up to five oral syringes of medicine every day for his epilepsy. They are lifesaving drugs, and it is essential that he swallows the medicine twice a day. He has a long history of severe sensory difficulties, and oral aversion prevented him from weaning and drinking normally for a long time. Consequently, taking those medicines was problematic. He struggled, pushed away, was like a ninja in his blocking skills, turned his head away, and, if we did get it in his mouth, he would spit, gag, scream. It was a complete nightmare. I'm ashamed to admit that desperation and concern made us pin our little boy down and force-feed it to him. We didn't know of any other option—until we found TAGteach! We started thinking about how we could break this down for him so taking medicine is not traumatic. We decided to start with "touch." Touching the syringe was okay. Not too scary. We used tickles and songs for the reinforcement after the tag to keep the task fun and silly and lighthearted. After "touch" was acceptable, we moved on to "hold." Getting him to hold the syringe gave him a sense of control. He must've known what was next and put the syringe to his own mouth. (We clicked!) We'd captured "taste." So, we practiced that for a while. We added songs he loved as reinforcement. He loved to hear me repeat phrases and lines of songs, and he quickly realized he could control my singing just by putting this thing in his mouth! He was in charge of his reinforcers.

I was a little worried about the next step. I had to add a squirt of the syringe into his mouth. With my hand over his, I pushed the tiniest amount medicine from the syringe into his mouth and reinforced heavily. Next, I reinforced for "swallow." The whole complex task of receiving and swallowing medicine had been broken down into small steps—steps that he had at least some control over. The rest is history!

He now takes his medicine like a champ, and all our lives are so much better for it. We currently don't need to click and reinforce every time he takes his medicine, but sometimes we fall back on it if he is having a particularly tricky time and his sensory issues are heightened. We can go back to "hold," or even right back to "touch."

This new trick has also massively improved his diet. We can use these steps to try new foods that have unfamiliar textures. My son went from being so orally aversive—there were days he wouldn't eat at all—to trying sushi, curry, and all sorts of things!

I believe the tag points of "touch," "hold," and "taste" are very effective for overcoming oral aversion and sensory issues. The process removes the anxiety associated with sensory overload and allows the child to have control over the delivery of food/medicine.

I have no idea what we would have done without TAGteach. I suspect we would still be pinning him down. Or maybe he would have wound up with a gastrostomy tube. I am sure you can imagine the relief we felt when we found a way of helping our son.

9.2   TAGteach Tale: Thinking for Creating Active Rather than Passive Learners

Ann Aiko Bergeron,
Morse-Alumni Distinguished Professor of
Theatre and Dance,
University of Minnesota, Duluth

Using TAGteach is great fun. Students always ask, "Can we tag today?" or confirm, "We need to tag the passé in the pirouette!" and on and on. But success for tagging physical skills is already well documented. As a teacher of adult pre-professionals, I had new questions.

How can I adapt the work so students don't depend on me to tag them all the time, and how can these concepts be reshaped to help them in the future when they move on into the professional world? How can TAGteaching shape detail beyond basic skills that transform dance technicians into dance artists?

And so, I introduced the concept of TAG thinking to my students. I think the best part about it is that it has taught the dancers to be very active, thinking learners, rather than passive, "teach me, teacher" machines.

After learning the concepts of TAGteaching in a practical, audibly tagged manner, the students learn to establish their own tag points and approximations. At first, I might offer them a list of choices, but eventually, they become extremely observant of their own actions and are able to self-impose tag points that I could not have ever perceived!

"The trick is to choose a goal just beyond your present abilities to target the struggle. Thrashing blindly doesn't help. Reaching does." Sound familiar?

Since integrating TAGteaching and TAG thinking, every day in the classroom is exhilarating for me. I have seen so many young people find their confidence and personal voices, not only as artists, but more importantly, as human beings.
Quotes from my students:

"My mindset changed during this course from fearing I would do something incorrectly to knowing I could make a mistake but that I knew exactly what to do to make it better. TAG thinking has enabled me to grow as a dancer because I am able to make mistakes and move past them. It allows us to use our intuition and trust ourselves when performing a move. Trust your body; trust that you're able to succeed by tweaking that one detail each time you perform it."

"TAG thinking has been a huge aspect of my new way of thinking. It is so great to find a particular area to focus on while doing a routine. It is even more gratifying when I 'mark' myself for being able to do it. This way of thinking is revolutionary by eliminating frustrations with dance and turning them into tag points, or goals."

10 Your Turn!

The instructions are...

10.1 Nagging? It's Just No Longer Necessary

Getting started is easy.

In fact, people who have attended the first day of a TAGteach workshop often come back the second day chronicling all they accomplished in just a few hours after class.

"I taught my daughter to tie her shoes in fifteen minutes!"

"I created five new tag points for my classroom students!"

"I thought about it and I've got three perfect tag points for improving presentations skills at work."

One attendee was excited to tell us how she managed her shyness at the hotel where she was staying for a two-day TAGteach workshop.

"I've always been shy around people and I try not to make eye contact in unfamiliar places. But after class yesterday, I made a focus funnel for myself.

The instructions are: when you pass someone in the hotel lobby, say hello.

The tag point is: say hello.

I kept the tagulator we made in the workshop clipped to my jacket and look—I pulled four beads! I can't believe it. I said 'hello' four times in under five minutes. That is huge for me!"

If you are beginning your TAGteach journey with this book, I recommend you start with an observation. Watch another teacher, coach, leader, or parent as they deliver information. This could be at a sports practice, in a classroom, at the office, at the dinner table, or even while watching TV. Consider if, and how, TAGteach would improve the environment for the teacher and/or the learner.

- Was the information delivered in a manner the learner could easily consume?
- Would a focus funnel help the teacher deliver the information?
- Would a tag point help the teacher create a well-defined criterion for success?
- Would a "tag" make the moment of success stand out for the learner?
- Was there any positive reinforcement that would improve the likelihood that success would happen again?

Once you're ready to use the tools with your learners, keep the explanation of the methodology brief.

It can be this quick and easy:

"First, I'll give you the instructions, and then I'll give you a single goal. That single goal is called a tag point. I'll tag with this sound (click, finger snap, or whatever you've chosen to mark success), so you'll know the instant the goal is met. Okay, let's give it a try!"

The instructions are: ...

The tag point is: ...

The type of reinforcement will depend on your learner. Remember, success to someone excited to learn is often reinforcing.

Final thoughts:

TAGteach was born from a need. I was a coach in need of a better teaching style with which to connect with my gymnasts to create long-term motivation and consistent success.

Nagging meant constantly asking the learner to come to me. I kept throwing my learners this rope—come to me. Here's the rope, grab it, and I'll pull you in. But that's the hard way, the long way.

The short way, the most effective way, is to go to the learner. Where are you? Let me go forward with you.

TAGteach allowed me to go to them. I left my stance, my position, my zone (which only divided us), and I joined them in their learning experience. TAGteach made the rope obsolete.

Now I use the **focus funnel** to gradually move toward my learner and when I arrive...

I use **tag points** to create small, incremental steps that encourage my learner to proceed with confidence.

I use **WOOF** to make sure those steps are clearly visible and sturdy beneath their feet.

I use **positive reinforcement** to increase the chance my students will be willing to take those steps in the future.

I use TAGteach to be a better teacher.

How will you use TAGteach?

For more information or to inquire about TAGteach workshops, certifications seminars, online courses, and presentations, please go to www.TAGteach.com

To contact Theresa Mckeon: t@TAGteach.com

To   contact   Joan   Orr: joan@TAGteach.com

Acknowledgments

To the remaining two-thirds of the original TAGteach vessel.

Joan: it's been a long and winding path that has taken us many places. We're not world-renowned (yet), but we've created another choice to make the teacher-learner dynamic more effective, and that is pretty cool. To your children, Anne and Jennifer: thank you for being test subjects and for becoming amazing TAGteachers. To your husband for his misguided support of your decision to leave a lucrative career to create TAGteach: Thanks, Dave!

Beth: from the first phone call when I said, "Hey, what do you think of this crazy idea..." and you responded, "Stop talking and let's do this already." To your son, Jake, for being a test subject who grew up to be a talented performer and just a cool guy.

To my children, Matthew and Katie, and my husband, Brian (the most supportive man I've ever known): you are my whole world and all that jazz, but, in regard to this journey, you were the original test subjects. Without you, there would be no TAGteach. But all kidding aside, you have become the very essence of what TAGteachers should be, and I'm in awe. And yes, Matthew, you get credit for the word "tagulator."

To those who linked with us to form TAGteach International LLC: Karen Pryor—without you, we would have been a boat without a sail; Aaron Clayton—you saw the potential; Silent Partner—your silent support has made this all possible.

Thank you, Julie S. Vargas, Ph.D., for your support and the many times you chaired our panels and presentations. To Alexandra Kurland for writing a clicker book about horses. To Jesús Rosales-Ruiz, Ph.D. for taking the time. To Susan G. Friedman, Ph.D. for the final scientific language.

Thank you to the first gymnasts (Ashley Dunlap), who said, "Sure! Sounds like a game," and to the coaches who said, "Give it a try." To

Rocky S. and Suzie S. for being open-minded and allowing clickers in your gyms—thank you. To the Oakville Butterflies, the first Special Olympics rhythmic gymnastics team to make use of the techniques and, especially, to the five-time Olympic gold medal winner Emily Boycott and her coach, Debbie Boycott—thank you for your commitment and dedication.

A million thanks to those who shared their TAGteach tales, so we could see the techniques working in a myriad of applications: Cheryl Anderson, Mary Lynch Barbera, Laura VanArendonk Baugh, Ann Bergeron, Sara Berry, Eva Bertilsson, Lisa Cerasoli and daughter Jazz Weaver (12), Lynette Cole, Karin Coyne, Abigail Curtis, Virginia Dare, Kelly Drifmeyer, Amy Duz, Katie Scott-Dyer, Victoria Fogel, Martha Gabler, Sara Geary, Keri Gorman, Tia Guest, Glenn Hughes, Joey Iversen, Dr. Martin Levy, Michele Karen McClean, Matthew McKeon, Pouliot, McLoudrey, Jim Mernin, Tim Meintz, Charlene Nelson, Sean Pogson Linda Randall, Tayja Jhane Sallie, Robin Sallie, Colleen Stalf, Brenda Terzich, Laura Monaco Torelli, Emelie Johnson Vegh, Bethan Mair Williams, Women at Fluvanna: Theresa, Tracey, Denise, and Janice.

To early adopters who added so much to the fold that they became the first TAGteach faculty: Eva Bertilsson, Patrice Robert, Luca Canever, Abigail Curtis, Karin Coyne, Martha Gabler, Keri Gorman, Joey Iversen, Francine Legault, Claudia Moser, Charlene Behr Nelson, Emelie Johnson Vegh, Anne Wormald—thank you all so much.

To those who kept my writing attempts out of the trash can: Marjie Alonso, Bryan Nelson, Miranda Hersey Helin, and my amazing final editor, Lisa Cerasoli, and her associate, Lauren Michelle Smith, at 529 Books—thank you and thank you and thank you.

Of course, there are so many others that built TAGteach over the years, it's impossible to thank them all.

To all of the dedicated teachers, parents, coaches, and leaders who continue to bring TAGteach where it is needed, I thank you.

TAGteach Reference List

Recent Article

1. "Positive Reinforcement Helps Surgeons Learn," *Scientific American*, online version, Lindsey Konkel on March 9, 2016. https://www.scientificamerican.com/article/positive-reinforcement-helps-surgeons-learn/

Peer Reviewed Published Studies

1. Fogel, V., Wiel, T.M. and Burns, H. (2010) Evaluating the Efficacy of TAGteach as a Training Strategy for Teaching a Golf Swing. J Behav Hlth Med 2010 (1): 24-41. http://www.scribd.com/doc/34776342/VFogel-JBHM-Golf-Study

2. Harrison, M.H. and Pyles, D.A. (2013) The Effects of Verbal Instruction and Shaping to Improve Tackling by High School Football Players. J Appl Behav Anal 46: 518-212. http://www.TAGteach.com/Resources/Documents/football%20TAGteach%202%20JABA%20Aug%202013.pdf

3. Levy. I.M., Pryor, K.W. and McKeon, T.R. (2015) Is Teaching Simple Surgical Skills Using an Operant Learning Program More Effective Than Teaching by Demonstration? Clinical Orthopaedics and Related Research. https://www.ncbi.nlm.nih.gov/pubmed/26369658

4. LaMarca, K., Gevirtz, R., Lincoln, A.J. et al. J Autism Dev Disord (2018). https://doi.org/10.1007/s10803-018-3466-4. Facilitating Neurofeedback in Children with Autism and

Intellectual Impairments Using TAGteach.
https://goo.gl/nf1q6P

5. Persicke, A., Jackson, M. and Adams, A.N. (2014) Brief Report: An Evaluation of TAGteach Components to Decrease Toe-Walking in a 4-Year-Old Child with Autism. J Autism Dev Disord 44:965-968. http://link.springer.com/article/10.1007%2Fs10803-013-1934-4

6. Pineda, J.A., Friedrich, E.V.C and LaMarca, K. (2014) Neurorehabilitation of social dysfunctions: a model-based neurofeedback approach for low and high-functioning autism. Front. Neuroeng 7: doi: 10.3389/fneng.2014.00029. http://journal.frontiersin.org/Journal/10.3389/fneng.2014.00029/full

7. Quinn, M.J., Miltenberger, R.G. and Fogel, V.A. (2015) Using TAGteach to Improve the Proficiency of Dance Movements. J Appl Behav Anal 48:11-24. http://onlinelibrary.wiley.com/doi/10.1002/jaba.191/pdf

8. Stokes, J.V., Luiselli, J.K., Reed, D.D. and Fleming, R.K. (2010) Behavioral Coaching to Improve Offensive Line Pass-Blocking Skills of High School Football Athletes. J Appl Behav Anal 43: 463-472. http://www.ncbi.nlm.nih.gov/pmc/articles/PMC2938948/

Published Books that Have Significant References to TAGteach

1. Bertillson, E. and Johnson Vegh. 2010. Agility Right from the Start: The ultimate training guide to America's fastest-growing dog sport. Karen Pryor Clicker Training, Sunshine Books Inc. http://amzn.to/1SCs310

2. Gabler, M. (2013). Chaos to Calm: Discovering Solutions to the Everyday Problems of Living with Autism. TAGteach International, Waltham MA.

http://amzn.to/1LuC4OZ
http://autismchaostocalm.com/expert-reviews/

3. Pryor, K.W. (2009) Reaching the Animal Mind: Clicker Training and What It Teaches Us About All Animals. Scribner, New York, NY.
    http://amzn.to/1BehY7v

4. Vargas, J.S. (2009) Behavior Analysis for Effective Teaching. Routledge Taylor and Francis Group, New York, NY.
    http://amzn.to/1Bei5QH

Published Review Articles that Mention TAGteach

1. Binder, C. Building Fluent Performance: Measuring Response Rate and Multiplying Response Opportunities. Behavior Analyst Today. 2010. 11:214-225
    http://files.eric.ed.gov/fulltext/EJ937632.pdf

Graduate Theses

1. Altman, L.D. Using Acoustical Feedback to Improve Elementary School Student Behavior during Transitions (2015). *Graduate Theses and Dissertations.*
    http://scholarcommons.usf.edu/etd/5443

2. Andrews, J.S. (2014) Evaluating the Effectiveness of TAGteach for Teaching Yoga Postures to Novice Yoga Practitioners. Master's Thesis in Child and Family Studies. University of South Florida.
    http://scholarcommons.usf.edu/cgi/viewcontent.cgi?article=6367&context=etd

3. Boggs, M.A. (2012) Using TAG to Increase Play Skills. Honors Thesis in Psychology, Western Michigan University.

http://scholarworks.wmich.edu/cgi/viewcontent.cgi?article=2574&context=honors_theses

4. Culloty, H. (2013) Comparison of Two Teaching Techniques in Improving Acquisition and Fluency of Math Skills. Master's Thesis in Applied Behavior Analysis. Bangor University. https://goo.gl/ctFMzZ

5. Ferguson, T.E. (2014) Using Auditory Feedback to Improve the Performance of Judokas during Uchi Komi. Master's Thesis in Communication Sciences and Disorders. University of South Florida. https://goo.gl/m8WQR8

6. Germino, A.E. (2013) Evaluating the Effects of TAGteach on the Rate of Learn Units Delivered to Students by Behavioral Therapists in a Center Based Program. Master's Thesis in Psychology. College of Science and Mathematics, California State University, Fresno. https://goo.gl/UszGst

7. Hester, S.E. Keeping Up with the Grandkids: Using TAGteach to Train Baton Twirling Skills in Older Adults (2015). Graduate Theses and Dissertations.
    http://scholarcommons.usf.edu/etd/5702

8. James, T. J. Using Auditory Feedback to Improve Dance Movements of Children with Disabilities (2015). Graduate Theses and Dissertations.
    http://scholarcommons.usf.edu/etd/5708

9. Quinn M.J. (2013) Using TAGteach to Enhance Proficiency in Dance Movements. Master's Thesis in Child and Family Studies. University of South Florida.
    http://scholarcommons.usf.edu/cgi/viewcontent.cgi?article=5948&context=etd

Presentations and Unpublished Studies

1. Barbera, M.L. (2010) The Use of TAGteach to Improve the Acquisition of Instruction Following in Children with Autism. In T. McKeon (Chair) and J. Vargas (Discussant): Recent Findings Using TAGteach in Diverse Populations and Applications Such as Autism and Commercial Fishermen. Symposium conducted at the Association for Behavior Analysis International 36th Annual Convention, San Antonio, TX.
   http://www.scribd.com/doc/32460984/TAGteach-and-Autism-blue

2. Benedetto-Nasho, E. and Cauley, K. (2011) Marking what You Want: Using TAGteach with Children with Autism. In T. McKeon (Chair) and J. Vargas (Discussant): Bridging the Gap Between Response and Reinforcement. Symposium conducted at the Association for Behavior Analysis International 37th Annual Convention, Denver, CO.
   http://www.TAGteach.com/Resources/Documents/ABAI%202011%20abstracts.pdf

3. Bishop J. (2012) Taming the Chatroom Bob: The role of brain-computer interfaces that manipulate prefrontal cortex optimization for increasing participation of victims of traumatic sex and other abuse online. In: 13th International Conference on Bioinformatics and Computational Biology (BIOCOMP'12), 16-19 July 2012, USA.
   http://www.scribd.com/doc/137448203/Taming-the-Chatroom-Bob-The-role-of-brain-computer-interfaces-that-manipulate-prefrontal-cortex-optimization-for-increasing-participation-of-victims

4. Boat, B. and Loar, L.M. (2004) Interactive Animal Assisted Therapy for Children and Families at Risk. In Pryor, K.W. (Chair) and Rosales-Ruiz, J. (Discussant): International

Symposium - Marker-Based Shaping ("Clicker Training") for Human Subjects: Three Ongoing Programs. Symposium conducted at the Association for Behavior Analysis International 30th Annual Convention, Boston, MA. http://www.TAGteach.com/Resources/Documents/ABAI%202 004%20abstracts.pdf

5. Canever, L, Casarini, F. and Galanti, E. (2014) The Effects of Using TAGteach to Promote Earthquake Safety for Children in School. Presented at the 7th Conference of the European Association for Behaviour Analysis. University of Stockholm. Stockholm, Sweden. Sept 10-13, 2014.
    http://www.europeanaba.org/events/submission/7/62
    http://TAGteach.blogspot.ca/2014/09/the-effects-of-using-TAGteach-to.html

6. Cauley, K.S. (2010). Shaping Up! The benefits of TAGteach and clicker training. Presented at the Ontario Association for Behavior Analysis Annual Conference, Toronto, ON.
    http://www.ontaba.org/pdf/newsletter/ONTABA%20Analyst %20(2011)%20Vol.%2017%20(1).pdf

7. Cauley, K. and Benedetto-Nasho, E. (2011) That's It! The Use of Acoustical Markers to Improve Student Responding. In T. McKeon (Chair) and J. Vargas (Discussant): Bridging the Gap Between Response and Reinforcement. Symposium conducted at the Association for Behavior Analysis International 37th Annual Convention, Denver, CO.
    http://www.TAGteach.com/Resources/Documents/ABAI%202 011%20abstracts.pdf

8. Cauley, K. and Benedetto-Nasho, E. (2010) the Combined Effects of TAGteach and Precision Teaching on Learning for Children with Autism. In T. McKeon (Chair) and J. Vargas (Discussant): Recent Findings Using TAGteach in Diverse Populations and Applications Such as Autism and Commercial Fishermen. Symposium conducted at the Association for Behavior Analysis International 36th Annual Convention, San Antonio, TX.

http://www.scribd.com/doc/32489101/TAGteach-and-Precision-Teaching-2010

9. Clark, J.W., Kuestner, D.A and Gerontes-Bowe, L. (2008) Outcomes of Alternative Strategies: TAGteach Process and Implementation Across Learning and Home Environments. Presented at the Autism Society of America 39th Conference. Scottsdale, AZ.
    https://asa.confex.com/asa/2008/techprogram/S3552.HTM

10. Fogel, V. (2005) TAGteaching in the Classroom. In Vargas, E.A. (Chair): TAGteaching: Current Practices in a Reinforcement-Based Teaching System. Symposium conducted at the 23rd Annual Western Regional Conference, California Association for Behavior Analysis, Dana Point, CA.

11. Fogel, V., Montgomery, J.L., Kosarek, J.A., Manzolillo, T., Bracero, V.M. and Howland, A.M. (2007) Feedback via Auditory Marker to Improve Task Analyzed Components of Caregiver Skills. In J.L. Montgomery (Chair) and Ragnarsson, R.S. (Discussant): International Symposium - Three Diverse Applications or Teaching with Acoustical Guidance (TAG): Caregivers, Juvenile Delinquents and Gymnasts. Symposium conducted at the Association for Behavior Analysis International 33rd Annual Convention, San Diego, CA.
    http://www.TAGteach.com/Resources/Documents/ABAI%202007%20abstracts.pdf

12. Gaw, M.R. (2014) Teaching with Acoustical Guidance: TAGteach. Workshop Presented at the 10th Annual Conference of the Hawaii Association for Behavior Analysis. Oct 24, 2014.

13. Gaw, M.R. and Dillenburger, K. (2014) Using 'TAGteach' as a teaching tool for Autism Spectrum Disorder. Presented at: Improving Children's Lives: An International Interdisciplinary Conference. Queen's University, Belfast, Northern Ireland. February 20–22, 2014.

http://www.iclconference.org/dloads/ICL-Conference-
Programme.pdf

14. Gaw, M.R. (2013) Using 'TAGteach' as a teaching tool for ASD. In R. M. Gaw (Chair) Session 2. Evidenced Based Practice for Participation and Inclusion. 3rd QUART Conference, Queen's University, Belfast, Sept 20, 2013. https://goo.gl/LUWYvd

15. Gorman, K. (2007) Teaching with Acoustical Guidance: Effects with the Juvenile Delinquent Population. In J.L. Montgomery (Chair) and Ragnarsson, R.S. (Discussant): International Symposium - Three Diverse Applications or Teaching with Acoustical Guidance (TAG): Caregivers, Juvenile Delinquents and Gymnasts. Symposium conducted at the Association for Behavior Analysis International 33rd Annual Convention, San Diego, CA. https://goo.gl/zYPFcg
http://www.tagteach.com/Resources/Documents/ABAI_2007
abstracts.pdf

16. Gutierrez, R. (2007) Tagging Imitation Skills of Students Diagnosed with Autism. Personal Communication, Applied Behavior Analysis Inc.
https://goo.gl/cn3Zym

17. Hahn, S. (2012) An Application of TAGteach to Teach Mobility Skills. In T. McKeon (Chair) and J. Vargas (Discussant): Recent Findings Using TAGteach in Diverse Populations and Applications in the Public School Setting. Symposium conducted at the Association for Behavior Analysis International 38th Annual Convention, Seattle, WA. https://goo.gl/eFqRp8

18. Hennessey, J. (2012) Ensuring Fidelity of Implementation After Obtaining Primary Level TAGteach Certification. In T. McKeon (Chair) and J. Vargas (Discussant): Recent Findings Using TAGteach in Diverse Populations and Applications in the Public School Setting. Symposium conducted at the Association for Behavior Analysis International 38th Annual Convention, Seattle, WA. https://goo.gl/HzKW1g

19. Johnson, K.A. (2008) Teaching Eye-contact in Response to a Peer's Initiation Using TAGteach Peer Tutoring. In T. McKeon (Chair) and J. Vargas (Discussant): An Analysis of the Effectiveness of Using an Acoustical Marker (TAG) on the Acquisition of Various Skills in Children with Autism and Other Developmental Disabilities. Symposium conducted at the Association for Behavior Analysis International 34th Annual Convention, Chicago, IL. https://goo.gl/V9bXRj

20. Loar, L.M. (2004) Training Adult Beginners to Figure Skate. In Pryor, K.W. (Chair) and Rosales-Ruiz, J. (Discussant): International Symposium - Marker-Based Shaping ("Clicker Training") for Human Subjects: Three Ongoing Programs. Symposium conducted at the Association for Behavior Analysis International 30th Annual Convention, Boston, MA. https://goo.gl/bLWBCY

21. Madden, K. and Hanson, R. (2006). The Use of TAG for Children with Autism. Personal communication: Applied Behavior Consultants Inc. https://goo.gl/jhvN4n

22. Maendler, R.L. (2009) An Auditory Marker as a Secondary Reinforcer in the Shaping of Specific Behaviors in Children with Autism. In T. McKeon (Chair) and J. Vargas (Discussant): Recent Findings on the Use of TAGteach in Children with Autism. Symposium conducted at the Association for Behavior Analysis International 35th Annual Convention, Jacksonville, FL. https://goo.gl/EkpTXL

23. McKeon, T. (2011). Using Shaping and Student Success to Increase Reinforcement for Teachers. In T. McKeon (Chair) and J. Vargas (Discussant): Bridging the Gap Between Response and Reinforcement. Symposium conducted at the Association for Behavior Analysis International 37th Annual Convention, Denver, CO. https://goo.gl/tnsaQn

24. McKeon, T. (2010) Creating and Following Instructions in Hazardous Situations - TAGteach on the Bering Sea. In T. McKeon (Chair) and J. Vargas (Discussant): Recent Findings Using TAGteach in Diverse Populations and Applications Such as Autism and Commercial Fishermen. Symposium conducted at the Association for Behavior Analysis International 36th Annual Convention, San Antonio, TX. https://goo.gl/raZTof

25. McKeon, T. (2007) Teaching Gymnastics Skills with an Acoustical Marker. In J.L. Montgomery (Chair) and Ragnarsson, R.S. (Discussant): International Symposium - Three Diverse Applications or Teaching with Acoustical Guidance (TAG): Caregivers, Juvenile Delinquents and Gymnasts. Symposium conducted at the Association for Behavior Analysis International 33rd Annual Convention, San Diego, CA. https://goo.gl/ZRpYJW

26. McKeon, T., Cauley, K.S., & Benedetto-Nasho, E. (2010). Does Everybody Understand? Using TAGteach to deliver clear instructions and positive reinforcement in a variety of applications. Workshop presented at the International Association for Behavior Analysis Annual Convention, San Antonio, TX. https://goo.gl/cMvcZX

27. Morien, M. and Eshleman J. (2010) The Effects of TAGteach Methods on Sign Language Object-Naming Skills in Non-Vocal Children with Autism. Chicago School of Professional Psychology. Poster Presentation. Association for Behavior Analysis International 36th Annual Convention, San Antonio, TX. https://goo.gl/3yrae6
http://www.scribd.com/doc/33974647/Morien-ABAI-2010s

28. Orr, J. and McKeon, T. (2004) Training Young Athletes with Positive Reinforcement and a Click Sound Marker Signal. In Pryor, K.W. (Chair) and Rosales-Ruiz, J. (Discussant): International Symposium - Marker-Based Shaping ("Clicker Training") for Human Subjects: Three Ongoing Programs. Symposium conducted at the Association for Behavior

Analysis International 30th Annual Convention, Boston, MA. https://goo.gl/VAZH5a

29. Roughton, A. & Cauley, K.S. (2012). Using targets to hit goals: Benefits of TAGteach and Target Training. Presented at the Ontario Association for Behavior Analysis Conference, Toronto, ON. https://goo.gl/u82NbA

30. Smith, S. and Hennessey J. (2012) Applying the Principles of TAGteach in a Public School Setting. In T. McKeon (Chair) and J. Vargas (Discussant): Recent Findings Using TAGteach in Diverse Populations and Applications in the Public School Setting. Symposium conducted at the Association for Behavior Analysis International 38th Annual Convention, Seattle WA. https://goo.gl/e9AaGd

31. Ueda. (2006). TAGteach Research at Applied Behavior Consultants Inc. Personal communication. http://TAGteach.com/Resources/Documents/Maris_PPT.pdf

32. Wasano, L. C. (2008). An Evaluation of Treatment Procedures For Increasing Social Skills: A case study. Personal Communication, STE Consultants. https://goo.gl/WDBduU

33. Wasano, L.C. and Trautman-Eslinger, S.E. (2008) Evaluating the Influence of TAGteach in Increasing Self-Help Skills with Individuals with Severe Developmental Disabilities. In T. McKeon (Chair) and J. Vargas (Discussant): An Analysis of the Effectiveness of Using an Acoustical Marker (TAG) on the Acquisition of Various Skills in Children with Autism and Other Developmental Disabilities. Symposium conducted at the Association for Behavior Analysis International 34th Annual Convention, Chicago, IL. https://goo.gl/fyykH6 http://www.tagteach.com/Resources/Documents/ABAI 2008 abstracts.pdf

34. Weiss, J. and Libby, M. E. (2008). Demonstration of the Effectiveness of Using a TAG to Promote Skill Acquisition for

Students with Autism. In T. McKeon (Chair) and J. Vargas (Discussant): An Analysis of the Effectiveness of Using an Acoustical Marker (TAG) on the Acquisition of Various Skills in Children with Autism and Other Developmental Disabilities. Symposium conducted at the Association for Behavior Analysis International 34th Annual Convention, Chicago, IL. https://goo.gl/WHNSvc

Don't Nag ... TAG!
Success the First Time with TAGteach®